Relationship

Facts, Trends, and Choices

Enhanced Edition

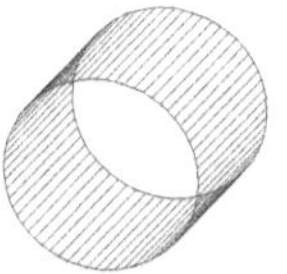

Author's Books

(As of June 20, 2020)[*]

Non-fiction

The Nature of Love and Relationships 2011, **2016**
Doubts and Decisions for Living:
  Volume I: The Foundation of Human Thoughts **2014**
  Volume II: The Sanctity of Human Spirit **2014**
  Volume III: The Structure of Human Life **2014**
Relationship Facts, Trends, and Choices **2016**
The Mysteries of Life, Love, and Happiness **2016**
Marriage and Divorce Hardships **2016**
Gender Qualities, Quirks, and Quarrels **2016**
Relationship Needs, Framework, and Models **2016**
Being Better Beings **2020**

Fiction

Persian Moons 2007, **2016**
Midnight Gate-opener 2011, **2016**
My Lousy Life Stories **2014**
Persian Suns **2021 (Planned)**

---

[*]12 older books are Enhanced Editions and printed in 2020. They were resubmitted to the Library and Archives Canada Cataloguing as well. If a book's 'print date' on the copyright page is older, the newest version is available at Amazon and bookstores.

Love and Relationships Series
1

Relationship

Facts, Trends, and Choices

(The Bottomline)

Tom Omidi, Ph.D.

Love and Relationships Series # 1

Omidi, Tom, 1945-
Relationship facts, trends, & choices : the bottomline
/ Tom Omidi.

(Love and relationships series ; 1)
ISBN 978-1-988351-04-9 (paperback)

1. Man-woman relationships. 2. Interpersonal relations.
3. Love. 4. Interpersonal conflict. 5. Couples. 6. Couples
Psychology. I. Title.

Old edition at
Library and Archives Canada Cataloguing in Publication
HQ801.O454 2016 306.7 C2016-902404-0

Published by Eros Books,
Vancouver, British Columbia
Canada

erosbooks2020.@gmail.com

Enhanced and Printed in 2020

Table of Contents

Introduction
The Bottomline
about Humans' Inability to Relate

About 1,000 facts, trends, and choices about marriage and love in this book demonstrate the difficulty of satisfying these basic human needs in the new era. With our weird perceptions and expectations from our marriages, we have gotten ourselves trapped in a web of complex dilemmas with agonizing results. All along, we are proving humans' general inability to relate or build peaceful environments due to our poor nature mixed with many idiotic modern mottos and values. Before getting into all these details, however, the following main fact, trend, and choice reveal the bottomline:

The Main Fact

Our understanding of love and relationships is wrong.

The Main Trend

Relationship conflicts have gotten out of hand
and the situation will continue to worsen.

The Main Choice

Only a drastic change in our mentalities can save the
future of relationships and alleviate human pains.

Here it is!—the grim bottomline about love and relationships amongst humans. Unless a person truly senses and agrees with this perspective, reading this book would prove of little value to him/her, although it might at least amuse him/her with some radical views about relationships and love, anyway. Then again, sticking adamantly to customary relationship solutions would not help our marriages, either. Looking for quick solutions or an ideal partner would only heighten one's inner conflicts and anxiety, as one moves vainly from one relationship to the next. Only by realizing the roots of current marital issues sincerely, one might find the wisdom and courage to build a productive, peaceful lifestyle with or without a partner.

Therefore, ask yourself, now and after reading the book, if you are convinced to change so many facets of your mentality gradually and painstakingly. Patience and faith is required to rebuild a constructive and manageable marital atmosphere, or alternatively develop a productive single life resolutely, as an ingenious, practical option. Sadly, most of us often fail in our relationship endeavours due to our naïve views and attitudes towards this contentious social issue. We just keep pampering our misperceptions, and then wonder why our marriages feel so frustrating, while our sense of loneliness heightens, too.

The term relationship(s) in this book mainly refers to love and marriage, but also human relations overall, as applicable in some phrases. After all, humans' inability to relate is tainting their social and organizational relationships badly, too. In fact, this pandemic is threatening humans' instinctual incentive and ability to live altogether, mostly due to our naïve mindsets and dogmatism about our means of relating.

The Main Fact

Everybody assumes to know relationship facts and problems, as if born a marriage guru. We trust our gut feelings too much. We think our impressions from movies and fanciful ideologies are solid. We are adamant and arrogant about our viewpoints and strategies that can make our relationships work perfectly. The only big hurdle we see is, *naturally,* our partner's lack of good judgment, conscience, and compassion. Otherwise, our relationships can work fine, we believe *sincerely*! If only s/he stopped being so stubborn and selfish all the problems would be solved, we dictate arrogantly. However, these assumptions and beliefs are totally false and misleading. The reason is that our knowledge and analytical capacity regarding relationships are quite limited. Our emotional tendencies, social pressures, and egos always hinder our understanding of relevant factors important for the success of relationships.

Naturally, our goal is to bring compassion and peace to our relationships and lives. Yet, we end up causing ourselves more hassle since we do not grasp the main purposes of marriage, yet persist on some untenable, selfish expectations. All along, we do not know how to live independently, either, to elude the rising hassles of relationships. Thus, we get trapped in shallow marriages and pursue our dull lives aimlessly, while our corny, painful dreams about a soul mate raise our sense of loneliness.

Sometimes, we might magically go even one step further and convince ourselves courageously that time has come to mend our own mentality—instead of our partner's—to save our relationship. However, at the end we fail, because we do not realize the full scope of efforts and sacrifices required for revamping our mentality effectively. We do not recognize that developing a sense of deep commitment and enhancing our self-awareness demands enormous personal conviction and a gradual lifestyle change to accept and overcome our lifelong naïve assumptions, habits, and pomposity. It would be hard to change our mentality, since we should suddenly think outside the box, often against the alluring social values and norms.

Nevertheless, to make our lives easier at least, we should ultimately refine our views of relationships, individually and collectively, instead of blaming our partners for everything or leaving our relationships prematurely. This is the bottomline! Our present attitude towards relationships can actually lead to the demise of humanity as well, if most of us remain incapable of relating properly and helping one another. Only if enough people appreciate the need for a major change, we might be able to build a social system that supports a new, progressive vision of relationships. For one thing, we might agree to stress on teamwork and selflessness, instead of fake individualism, equality, and similar misleading criteria. We must define valid relationship purposes according to some basic guidelines and honour the sanctity of relationships as an independent entity with unique needs of its own.

Several hundred facts about relationships explained in this book support the *main fact* stated on Page 1. These facts must convince us, with a rather high urgency, that our pervasive relationship perceptions and practices only alienate us further and make future generations' life even harder. The trends in recent decades demonstrate these facts clearly. Accordingly, our choices at so many levels are rather obvious, too, if only we stop and think more practically. All the trends and choices discussed in this book are becoming painful, sad facts rapidly and overwhelming our lives more every day. They reveal our negligence about relationships' generic needs and our attitudes' irrationally in terms of imposing our demented personal needs on our relationships. **Our present perceptions of love and relationships are wrong.**

The Main Trend

Our marriages have been shaping around some shallow social values, showy lifestyles, and naive mottos that we have been embracing so keenly in recent decades. We have now become addicted to materialism, judge one another hastily according to superficial notions, and choose our partners based on wrong criteria and purposes. Even when we are less calculating or trust love to strengthen our relationship, we are incognizant of the right factors that make a relationship successful. We are unaware of the specific relationship needs that we should fulfil before stressing on our personal needs, including love. Instead, we sloppy humans have allowed many crooked social trends, including arrogance, competition, greed, fashion, and duplicity guide our personal needs as well as our rising expectations from relationships in recent decades.

Many other trends reflect our deteriorating mentalities and their impacts on societies: we seek quick fixes in all aspects of our lives without grasping the effects of our actions and plans for us and our kids. We dismiss the fact that our obsession to focus on our seemingly urgent, selfish needs sabotages the opportunity of building relationships and a practical social structure. We stress on our naive impressions of individuality to set our relationship parameters. We have all along tried to deal merely with the symptoms of relationship breakdowns, instead of looking for relationships' specific needs and their inherent problems in the new era. The trend is to trust our guts and maybe some raw social norms and juvenile mottos to set our tolerance level in relationships. We stress on living 'in the now,' rather than developing realistic guidelines for keeping relationships manageable and effective, which would boost personal and social peace as well.

Unfortunately, all the trends indicate that our relationships have become victims of social paradoxes growing fast in all aspects due to our pervasive superficial values and lifestyles. **Relationship conflicts have gotten out of hand and the situation will continue to worsen.**

The Main Choice

We should make many tough choices in life to stay sane and prosper as an independent person. Almost all those choices affect our views towards, and attitudes in, relationships. Some specific choices directly relate to our relationships as will be discussed in this book. Yet, all our choices about various life issues affect everybody and our relationships in some manner. The reason is that our values and needs dictate our mentalities and varied choices, including those related to our relationship issues and decisions.

Nevertheless, we should prepare ourselves to either live alone, at least mentally and emotionally, or learn novel means of keeping a civilized relationship with a relatively normal partner. We might have a rather good partner, but when we do not appreciate each other and do not know how to relate, the sense of loneliness would feel even more excruciating than the option of living alone. Nevertheless, the outcome of our life choices is that we develop a particular mentality to spend our lives with someone or alone. Accordingly, the bottomline is that we must prepare ourselves for a stoic life of semi-solitude supported by inner strengths and convictions whether we are in a relationship or not. However, for being in a relationship, we also need more patience and progressive mentalities for relating to our partners practically and constructively. A major catastrophe in society is that almost no one is following either of these options effectively. Nobody knows how to relate in a relationship constructively, or how to live as an independent person who enjoys his/her life of semi-solitude, satisfied with his/her own personal passions and thoughts. Therefore, **only a drastic change in our mentalities can save the future of relationships and alleviate our pains.**

This book consists of three parts: Facts, Trends, and Choices. The objective is to emphasize on itemized facts, conclusions, and the bottomline about the declining state of relationships in the new era for the readers who prefer this type of outlined presentation. Those interested in details and technical analyses are encouraged to read *The Nature of Love and Relationships* by this author.

Every one of the facts, trends, and choices noted deserves a deep scrutiny and many of them require long contemplations for remembering and raising our self-awareness about modern relationships' intricacies. Some of the points need independent studies and books by themselves to highlight how we could possibly make our lives more meaningful within or without a relationship. Accordingly, numbering the points has also been for goading the readers to pause and ponder the relevance and importance of each point at personal and social levels, rather than reading the passages quickly.

Facing the reality of life in modern societies is useful for keeping our sanity at least. Sadly, this reality is highly affected by the facts, trends, and choices enumerated in this book about relationships. Pondering these points might clarify so many topics that have been confusing us about relationships in the recent decades. Ironically, we have heard or noticed these sad facts about relationships and marital life, nowadays, but have not reflected upon them seriously, as we usually like to believe we are immune against these companionship traps and we are smart to run away if necessary.

An essential fact (negligence) in itself is that relationship requirements and realities are not taught at schools to prepare the public for this highly stressful personal challenge. Instead, society abuses people's knack for romanticism with mushy love stories and movies that ruin their basic senses regarding social life and marriage. Overall, people are quite unprepared intellectually and emotionally to make sound marital and life decisions.

Raising the public's interest regarding the declining state of relationships and offering a realistic and practical perspective about this social dilemma has been the main goal for writing this book with lots of research. Still, classifying and combining over thousand facts, trends, and choices to create a concise picture of relationships has been tough, while many subsidiary facts and details have been left out to keep this book short.

More urgently, however, the author's biggest hope has been to goad scholars and governments to devise better social values and principles that can help people build their families and survive longer in harmonic and peaceful environments. The way family relationships are damaging our societies and lives is hard to miss for any objective person. We can see how dysfunctional, costly, and stressful our approach towards this primary human need has been all along. The agonizing marital conflicts and divorces rising in all societies render clear proofs of our low interest and knowledge to address humans' basic need for companionship with such dire effects on personal health and social harmony.

PART I

Relationship Facts

Chapter One

Facts about

Our Mentalities

Some primary facts provide the platform for adjusting our mentalities about the nature and prospect of relationships these days. These alarming facts are especially important to ponder during courting period before getting married.

1. More than 50% of marriages in modern societies end up in divorce and separation.
2. Furthermore, a large population has difficulty even starting a relationship due to the complexity of building a common ground for relating.
3. Even among the couples who stay married, a good majority consider their relationships unsatisfactory or torturous. They simply tolerate the situation because they are sceptical about the consequences of ending their marginal relationships.
4. Most of us deliberately ignore the above three fundamental facts when we fall in love or feel desperate for a companion.
5. Naively, we prefer to dismiss the simple *fact* that so many marriage failures represent something fundamentally wrong with the way we perceive and handle relationships.
6. Due to many social deprivations, we actually feel too needy, nowadays, for a companion to mitigate our loneliness and relieve our other sources of suffering as well. This growing

neediness is much beyond our instinctual needs for mating and social belonging.

7. We have gradually come to view 'companionship' a basic need rather than a medium range social need. Most of us consider it the highest prize God bestows upon humans, not to mention the sexual privileges of relationships. This deep belief has evolved rather instinctually, but mostly through social conditioning in recent decades.
8. Combining the above seven facts, it becomes obvious that most people suffer in life due to relationships (whether they are in one or not), since having a companion feels like an essential need, especially when it often remains unfulfilled.
9. Meanwhile, couples do not develop the right temperament and proper guidelines to *relate* rather effectively.
10. The above facts also show that couples are not properly *trained* to perceive, build, and maintain their relationships.
11. In fact, couples cannot even anticipate the basic hurdles of relationships or assess them realistically.
12. All couples, especially newlyweds, have wrong perceptions about both the purposes and potentials of relationships. This general ignorance is especially harmful to people when they are either unconscious about the high likelihood of marriage breakdowns or prefer to dismiss this alarming fact.
13. Moreover, couples are not trained to work proactively from day one to protect their marriage from going astray. They are not aware of the need for monitoring their relationships' health routinely and the means of doing it.
14. Meanwhile, the old principles that kept marriages together are long gone and no new principles have been developed to keep couples alert in line with deeply stringent relationship needs in the new era.
15. As societies have become more complex, our lifestyles and expectations have changed drastically without realizing their long-term social effects and practicality. Accordingly, our relationships have become too hard to fathom and manage.

16. Our personal needs, insecurities, and idiosyncrasies have also been escalating in line with changes in social values. However, instead of appreciating the hazards of our rising personal flaws, we justify our new needs and mentalities so obsessively and often arrogantly.
17. On the other hand, we notice our partner's simplest flaws so quickly and nag about them impatiently.
18. We have difficulty accepting that people's personal defects are natural consequences of their genetic and upbringing conditions, mostly beyond their immediate control.
19. Therefore, we keep pushing our partners to change, or we retaliate to make them suffer.
20. At the same time, we are getting more obsessed every day about finding happiness and love in such a contaminated social environment.
21. We have become more demanding of our marriage partners, society, and ourselves in line with our growing neediness.
22. Our unrelenting personal needs, especially individualism, is placing undue pressure on relationships and causing more frictions.
23. Conversely, personal stress from relationships is putting big pressure on society and the economy, too.
24. In fact, social pressures make us needier for a companion, and in return, our failing relationships are ruining the social foundation. This vicious cycle is running out of control and making both society and individuals sicker and sadder every day.
25. Social mechanisms and laws are not useful anymore, either, to respond to the newer needs of relationships. Neither our religious guidelines, nor our legal systems protect couples or offer practical ways of relating in a complex environment we have created for ourselves and cherish blindly.
26. We dismiss the need for serious studies about relationships and their doomed path. Neither the public nor governments realize, or simply ignore, that family values are in need of a

major overhaul. We just appear nonchalant about humans' doomed destiny—unless we wish to admit nothing can be done regarding this looming catastrophe due to humans' flawed nature and rampant social immorality.

27. Actually, nobody seems to know how to go about finding solutions for our derailed societies and relationships. Thus, people seem resigned to rely solely on the natural course of history to correct the rotting situation of relationships. This approach, however, demonstrates only our wishful thinking that has no chance for success.

28. To address relationship issues, personal and governmental efforts are required for: 1) an overhaul of couples' mindset, and, 2) development of a set of practical guidelines to help people relate more effectively in their relationships. Why we ignore this simple fact is ironic and amazing. Or, at best, humans might have simply realized and admitted that they do not have the expertise or motivation to do anything about these clear facts. We have simply resigned and think, *Just let us hope for the best*

29. Obviously, we can never eliminate relationship conundrums fully due to humans' conflicting needs and instincts, egos, hormones, and gender differences. However, we can make relationships smoother by following some basic guidelines, while prepare ourselves more proactively for the inevitable hassles of relationships.

30. So far, we have ignored the need for radical solutions to make relationships more manageable in the new world.

31. We have failed to see the need for a new set of Generally Acceptable Relationship Principles (GARP) to match social changes in the new era.

32. Propagating GARP actively is mostly crucial for changing couples' mentalities about the nature of relationships and love and applying more civilized means of relating. Maybe we can witness some tangible results in a century, if by then humanity still exists in a functional way. Yet, even gradual

changes in social mentality can help us all in major ways immediately.

33. Creating a new atmosphere for relationships would not be easy and quick. People are not ready to quit their personal convictions and pleasures to improve their relationships. Yet, we must face this challenge soon to save humanity and our souls from so much suffering in relationships.
34. Ultimately, our personal goal is to clarify the true nature of love and relationships, so that we may come to terms with ourselves personally for a more tranquil life in or out of a relationship. Once we learn to live without expecting love and relationships bringing us that elusive happiness, we might begin to enjoy our relationships, too.

The bottomline is that:

A: We need to upgrade our mindsets

35. Both our initial optimism about relationships (when we start one) and subsequent retaliations (when it fails) are naïve and destructive.
36. Our perspective of relationships is too raw and incompatible with the format of modern societies. Mainly, we must lower our expectations from relationships in order to measure and attend to our rising personal needs independently.
37. We must prepare ourselves, emotionally and financially, to deal with the high possibility of failure in our relationships.
38. We must admit that only by conscious efforts and major personal sacrifices a relationship might survive. Our present mindsets (personal priorities) and social values make the job of prolonging our relationships extremely difficult, if not impossible altogether.

B. We must understand human limitations

39. The complexity of human cognition and behaviour, driven by so many personal needs, traits, and perceptions, causes all kinds of relationship problems.

40. The main causes of relationship failures remain beyond partners' control. In other words, partners cannot elude their developed personalities or improve themselves quickly and easily. They are helpless due to human's deep psychological defects and genetic built.
41. Our faultfinding attitude towards our partners is a worthless exercise. In addition, our efforts to change others (including our partners) are absurd, especially if the matter is pursued through retaliation and intimidation.

C. We urgently need new solutions and guidelines

42. Dynamic relationship principles are now needed to reflect the realities of the modern world, especially people's rising obsessions for independence, individualism, and sexuality.
43. New guidelines are needed to facilitate individuals' drive to be successful, assertive, proactive, and make the best use of their lives.
44. Revolutionary social mechanisms and norms are needed to help us manage our relationships and possibly reduce their chances of failure.
45. Dynamic social mechanisms and education are urgently needed to prepare couples for the psychological pressures of relationships, especially separation.
46. Radical laws must be devised to make separations easy and somewhat stress free.

Chapter Two

Facts about

Partners' Personalities

The combined effects of our vast superficial needs and the demand for social adaptation have made us phoney, and we have lost our abilities to feel and behave naturally. With our exaggerated identities and ideals, we do not know who we are.

47. The way we go about satisfying our personal needs portrays our 'personality.'

    Personality also *reveals*, i) our *efforts* to relate to people and the world, and, ii) other people's *perceptions* about our efforts to relate to them and the world. Meanwhile, both our and people's grasps of our personalities are quite erroneous in relation to our complex, concealed personalities.

48. Accordingly, 'personality' remains an abstract concept, as it is mostly a reflection of who we want to be or try to be, not the true person we are or can portray. And, since personality remains largely subject to crude judgments by other people about who we are, again not the person that we really are. In all, 'personality' remains a complex dimension of human with peculiar characteristics that are difficult to pinpoint or predict, let alone manage.

49. At the same time, personality is the main tool and motivator to go about satisfying our personal needs. Accordingly, our

fake identities often confuse our minds and the course of our lives completely.

50. Personality also contains a large inventory of emotions and cognition. Therefore, the shallow personalities that we try to adopt or imitate hurt us deeply, too.

51. We love *who we believe we are,* thus avoid any advice or clues about the way our personality is hurting us or people around us. Accordingly, we seldom give ourselves a chance to find out *who we are.*

52. Unfortunately, we hate to agree that our new values and our personalities are too ambiguous (and shallow too), and they are becoming drastically detrimental to our happiness and health, as well as our relationships.

53. The distinction between good and bad has become vastly subjective, nowadays. We rely on authorities, celebrities, and propagandas to measure good and bad. Our personalities evolve around the same values. Thus, defining and building balanced, useful personalities have become tough.

54. Accordingly, studying human personality, and its impact on our lives, has been highly urgent, because we are all striving to establish our identities both personally and collectively as confused humans. This knowledge can boost our personal lives as well as the quality of our relationships.

55. The personality model presented in all *relationships* books by this author and referred to throughout this book has three components:

- **Ego** reflects (and drives) our desires, ambitions, sense of responsibility, defence mechanism, and all other traits that enable us to assert ourselves and protect our lives.
- **Self** contains our inner urges, integrity, inquisitiveness, potentialities, love, creativity and spirituality. This aspect of our personality reflects humans' soul and vulnerability.
- **Model** is the most practical aspect of our personality in the way it tries to help us adapt to social norms and be

accepted and admired if possible. It is driven mainly by our conditional and adaptation needs.

56. Subject to our genetics and experiences, each individual's personality manifests by a different degree of Ego, Model, and Self.

57. We can make the following hypotheses about individuals' personality:

- Self is driven mostly by individuals' instincts and spirit.
- Ego is driven mostly by individuals' genetics, chemistry, and nervous system. However, Ego is also affected by conditioning and defence mechanisms.
- Model is driven mostly by individuals' conditioning and defence mechanisms as well as social environment.
- 'Human nature' is mostly a combination of Self and that part of Ego that is driven by genetics, chemistry, and nervous system.
- All three personality aspects, i.e., Self, Ego, Model, draw on person's cognition (logic) to manage a person's affairs

58. Therefore, personality can be identified and measured in terms of how effectively a person can:
    - apply his/her **instincts (Self)**,
    - reason and use his/her **logic**,
    - connect with people and society—**Model**, and
    - manage his **Ego** for his/her own benefit.

59. A unique mix of the above four factors makes up a person's personality and determines his effectiveness and charisma.

60. The complexity of our interactions and communications is due to the way different personality aspects of people react to one another in every situation without proper attention or intention.

61. Although we may apply any mix of the personality aspects in a special instance for a special purpose, we often adopt a

fixed personality profile that reflects a certain proportion of each aspect of personality.

62. Our actions and attitudes reflect some notion (degree) of all three aspects of our unique personalities. However, we can witness how every one of our daily interactions has a tone in line with one particular aspect of our personality.

63. People often behave under the influence of one of the main personality aspects, i.e., Ego, Self, and Model.

64. Our personality aspects create misperceptions when we are sending or receiving a message.

65. The irony is that we believe or pretend to be communicating always with total honesty and integrity. We believe we are communicating with our Self. However, in reality, almost all communications are contaminated by Ego and Model.

66. It helps our relationships, and life as a whole, if we learn to gauge and adjust the volume of these personality aspects regularly. We can make a habit to monitor and distinguish the personality aspects in our encounters and see which one is usually in control and why.

67. Keeping track of the interworking and manifestation of our personality aspects is the most important step towards self-awareness, which is obviously the best tool for improving our relationships as well.

68. All three personality aspects have both good and bad sides.

69. The three aspects of personality collectively drive people's communications without their sufficient awareness and compassion, thus they get offended during this process quite often. Therefore, it may help our relationships, and our lives as a whole, if we learn to gauge and adjust the volume of these personality aspects regularly.

70. A useful process for raising self-awareness, and minimizing relationship clashes as well, is to pursue the steps outlined in Appendix 12-A at the end of Chapter Twelve (Personality Aspects' Role).

71. The personality aspects, i.e., Self, Model, and Ego, reflect how we value and use the four personality factors, i.e., our instincts, logic, adaptability (model), and ego (self-defence.)
72. For building an ideal relationship, partners should be rather *good and enlightened* persons first.
73. A person's goodness mainly indicates his/her personality dominance. Obviously, the more a partner is driven by Self, and the less he/she is influenced by Ego, the better he/she is with a higher chance to build an ideal relationship, too. The excessive use of Model also taints one's personality mainly by making him/her too phony. Thus, goodness is a reflection of a person's level of naturalness and integrity.
74. In reality, though, most people are becoming more crooked, phony, spoiled, and demanding every generation, thus they are also becoming more incompatible with one another every day. Naturally, personality defects, insecurities, and evilness also reduce the relationships' chances of success drastically.
75. Naturally, genetics determines a good portion of a person's personality and destiny. Even his/her conscious attempts to revamp his/her personality cannot easily override the effects of genetics easily.
76. People also perceive the world and people according to their unique personalities. The dire effects of our perceptions and misperceptions on our relationships are vast as discussed in Chapter Seven.
77. Furthermore, it appears that men and women have inherent differences in terms of perceiving events and people. Each gender has a rather uniform way of interpreting the world and setting its priorities.
78. Overall, it seems that our fates are largely mapped for us in our genes. We think and act in certain ways that lead to a particular life path at last.
79. At the same time, culture always also plays a major role in the development and manifestation of gender differences.

80. Ultimately, however, we can play a role in strengthening our personalities and relationships regardless of the effects of nature, genes, and gender differences. We can do so by learning about our three personality aspects and raising our self-awareness in terms of our thoughts, feelings, and deeds, which in turn strengthen our characters and spirits.

Chapter Three

Facts about

Love and Happiness

We all strive to capture lasting happiness through love and companionship. In return, people's high expectations for love and happiness from their relationships have made especially their marriages too complex, unnatural, and impractical.

At the same time, now relationships play an essential role in people's psyches due to their naïve impressions about love and happiness. Thus, understanding this chapter's points about the natures of love and happiness can help our perceptions of relationships and boost their health substantially.

81. Love and happiness are two abstract concepts that we seek obsessively, nowadays, like two given human privileges. We also believe love brings us eternal happiness automatically.
82. At the same time, we imagine everybody can feel and find love easily and naturally. We see it as our basic entitlement!
83. Therefore, we have conditioned our brains to put too much value and trust in love. In addition, we have come to believe that love is the most reliable success factor for relationships. These are surely wrong ideas! Actually, love is normally a gigantic myth to stress upon, impose on relationships, or consider essential as a success factor.

84. We look for love and happiness in relationships, as we are programmed, instinctually and culturally, to think that a soul mate can relieve our loneliness and complete our identity.
85. Furthermore, we believe a good companion can *potentially* satisfy a wide range of our personal needs, including sex, compassion, and spiritual (selfless) love.
86. In a sense, we intuitively put too much faith in relationships' immense potentials. Thus, we remain naively hopeful about the likelihood of turning all that potentiality into reality—to make all those good things that we had imagined happen in our relationships, in addition to love.
87. Nevertheless, the outcome is that we seek happiness and love obsessively. Worse, we expect to find them externally, in our relationships and society, instead of looking for them within ourselves as a personal challenge and attribute, which could then also nurture our relationships.
88. We have not been able to be happy as individuals and we do not know anything about the path to happiness, either, so we look for a good relationship to do it for us. However, a 'relationship' is not a happiness-generating machine. Thus, we put high expectations on people, mainly our partners, to enliven our relationships and bring us happiness.
89. In all, we make our partners accountable for the happiness that a relationship is supposed to provide. Since our partners are looking for the same thing, our relationships face lots of pressures quickly. Instead of getting the kind of happiness and love we desire, we encounter our partners' demands to focus on making them happy—a total contrast to what we had initially assumed!
90. We ignore the high likelihood that our partners have not been able to make themselves happy (although, nowadays, everybody likes to shout how happy and mature they are and how beautiful life is). So, how can we expect them to make us happy? Are we naïve, or selfishly assume we can tame them to serve us?

91. Thus, partners play all kinds of games and roles to control and manipulate each other, and to feel loved and in charge of their relationship in hopes of finding a relative happiness.
92. Of course, sometimes, one partner submits to the whims of the other eventually, because he/she gets tired of fighting or playing games, or whatever. Yet, this type of relationship is doomed and unacceptable in our modern societies, anyway.
93. Happiness is a myth all by itself, but hoping to find it in our raw relationships is plain utopian—only a wishful thinking cultivated in our imaginations.
94. A major conflict and dilemma is that we want happiness to fit our immature lifestyles, instead of a lifestyle that could stir peace of mind as the closest state of happiness.
95. Unfortunately, human nature does not support happiness and tranquility, either, due to innate human urges for challenge, controversy, power, domination, rivalry, greed, struggle for survival, etc. Anger, hatred, jealousy, aggressiveness, and spite come to us so naturally, but we must try very hard to be honest, compassionate, sincere, etc.
96. Most relationships become instable fast, only because they fail to fulfil our fantastic desires for happiness and sexuality.
97. The slogan 'life's purpose is to find happiness' is causing more suffering than guiding people towards happiness. The reason is that it makes people believe that such a myth (happiness) actually exists, and it is merely due to their bad luck, stupidity, or relationships they cannot capture it.
98. The purpose of life is neither to find and spread happiness, nor to create good human beings. Life does not have any special meaning, nor is it about anything in particular. Life is merely a collection of events and moments that transpires in people's lives according to natural laws and chances and affects them based on their level of cognition.
99. Humans have many other ambitions in life that they usually pursue with greater passion than their desire for happiness or even pleasures, e.g., need for love, power, or recognition.

Most people just cannot sit idle and bask in some kind of contentment.

100. Happiness and goodness are the likely (automatic) results of succeeding to set the right balance between our ambitions and contentment.

101. The fact that we have to try so hard to become better human beings and find happiness is another clue that humans are not pure by nature, which then diminishes their abilities to build good relationships as well.

102. The simple fact that Ego is an inherent part of the human psyche is enough to cause selfishness, hypocrisy, bias, and hundreds of other impurities and flaws.

103. Obviously, love and happiness enrich people's lives, so they are relevant factors for grasping the meaning of life, too, but they must not turn into obsessions and distract our attention to the main success factors in relationships.

104. More importantly, however, love and happiness are highly related to a person's true nature, self-awareness, humility, and knowledge of who s/he is.

105. Human purity is not a matter of comparing the number of their good deeds versus bad ones, either, even if a bunch of people did more good than bad. Purity is an absolute fact, not an algebraic equation. It either exists or does not. The only question is how often humans' impurity approaches evilness. Too often and universally, it usually feels!

106. Presuming and propagating that humans are good by nature would only create a false expectation in society, and people would get even more disappointed and frustrated regularly when they face reality. The more we view people's malice as unnatural, the more deliberate their actions look and the more disappointed we feel, which is another fallacy in itself.

107. On the other hand, if we accept that humans are flawed and impure by nature, we would develop more tolerance and compassion, because we understand that human actions are mostly beyond their control or are triggered by greed and

social corruption. We might even smarten up and correct the social causes of human corruption.

108. Our reaction to people's claims of purity and happiness shows our major scepticism. We need a lot of evidence to believe in even one person's goodness and happiness.

109. Once we accept that human nature is impure, we would also keep our expectations from people and relationships low and realistic. We get less surprised and angry, since we develop some form of understanding and compassion towards our partners and the helpless humanity in general.

110. Nevertheless, we create deep conflicts in our relationships by our misperception about happiness being a phenomenon that someone else can bring to us. With this type of mindset, we should expect only more conflicts in our relationships and life in general. Actually, instead of love and happiness, we must expect antagonism and depression as natural traits of humans.

111. Another big misunderstanding is that relationships can solve our personal problems, which would then lead to happiness. This is another false assumption and an invalid expectation.

112. In fact, instead of expecting relationships solve our personal problems, we should expect and prepare ourselves to handle the added hardships of relationships and the high chance of separation with huge hassles of its own.

113. All the facts, trends, and choices noted in this book clearly stress the need for taming our needs for happiness and love, and instead focusing on building teamwork and tolerance for maintaining a sensible relationship.

114. Even when both partners have good natures and intentions, and realize that give and take in a relationship may provide a relative sense of comfort (not necessarily happiness) for both partners, they still do not know how to do it. They do not know how to *relate* fairly.

115. Therefore, a *relationship framework* and set of *principles* are needed to help partners relate with least frictions.

116. These relationship framework and principles should show couples how to run a simple relationship without putting too much demand on each other for irrelevant and impossible objectives, especially eternal love and happiness.

117. These relationship framework and principles should bring objectivity back into relationships.

118. The chance of finding happiness in relationships depends on many factors, mainly our mental ability to interpret, absorb, and reflect happiness. As a first step, we should admit that happiness is more a subjective perception than a tangible commodity to expect from relationships.

119. People behave neurotically and randomly to find happiness in a variety of things or events, like travelling, taking yoga lessons, shopping excessively, searching for love, dancing, getting into art, etc. However, these random searches for happiness or relief might cause only more frustration until we settle with our inner selves, grasp a realistic meaning for happiness, and relax naturally.

120. In fact, our efforts for finding love and happiness often stir extra psychological burdens, disappointment, and a sense of failure and loneliness.

121. Partners' personalities affect their perceptions of love and the way they strive to satisfy them. In fact, three types of love satisfy the three aspects of our personalities:

- **SLove** is Self driven and reflects our most spiritual and selfless way of loving someone.
- **ELove** is Ego driven and reflects our insecurities and dire deficiency need for love and attention.
- **MLove** is Model driven and reflects our most practical means of communicating our passion to another person without going overboard with our imaginary perceptions regarding the power of love and its importance for the success of our relationships.

122. People's uniqueness in using their three personality aspects (Ego, Model, and Self) also makes them perceive 'love' uniquely in their own ways and react to it differently, too.

123. The commonplace love consists of, i) physical attraction and lust, and, ii) a mix of the three types of love (SLove, MLove, and ELove). Accordingly, we can say that:
  - Seeking love reflects both our instinctual and conditional urges (mostly superficial needs).
  - The 'need for a companion' affects all three personality aspects (Ego, Model, and Self) of a person, while each personality aspect plays a role when someone expresses love to another person.
  - The meaning of love varies for each person depending on the level of Ego, Model, and Self he/she has applied to perceive love. Accordingly, each person is driven by a certain level of SLove, MLove, and ELove at the time he/she expresses his/her love.
  - Inventing an imaginary meaning for love (outside the meanings of SLove, ELove, MLove) and spreading it for common use is pointless—except for writing fiction and making movies.

124. On most occasions, our initial perception and impression of SLove fades away after we get into our relationships. The reason is simple: Self is needed to protect SLove. Besides, SLove deteriorates when partners' new perceptions about their relationship override their initial ones.

125. The complex 'need for a companion' comprises of many personal needs that extend over the full spectrum of the 'personal needs tree,' from the basic need for sex all the way to our high-level need for spirituality through SLove.

126. The main urges that drive humans to find a mate are Sex, Compassion, and SLove. Compassion by itself includes many other urges such as ELove, MLove, security, respect, dependence, and recognition.

127. Naively, we think that our partners are capable of fulfilling the full spectrum of our needs, including sex, compassion, and love, thus make us happy.

128. In reality, however, even the basic task of satisfying sex in relationships has become rather complex, because sex is now often treated as a regulating tool to tame our partners, instead of a basic need.

129. Furthermore, sexual deprivations have risen due to couples' drive for ELove (deficiency love) getting out of control.

130. With regard to compassion, couples are lacking the required qualities, too, to satisfy this complex need of humans. In fact, the supply and demand for compassion is imbalanced. People demand a lot of compassion from their relationships, but hardly have any themselves to share with their partners; or do not know how to go about showing it.

131. As noted before, it appears that we have created most of the medium-range personal needs (including compassion) rather superficially through evolution and according to cultural conditions. These mid-range needs are not natural like our basic need for sex (and the urge for reproduction, especially for women) and our high-level need for selfless, spiritual love (SLove), which are instinctual needs.

132. Thus, the need for compassion has become quite complex to understand and satisfy, too.

133. Accordingly, a big challenge in relationships is to learn about sharing compassion without imagining and expecting it as a requirement, especially in terms of our partners' full devotion and SLove (selfless love).

134. In terms of satisfying our personal need for love, we have the hardest time. While lots of ambiguity and complication surround the concept of love, our drive to find happiness through love is tough to curtail.

135. Yet, we cannot stop our search for that special person who can make our dreams come true. We hope to complete our existence through him/her. This lifelong crusade is partly

the symptom of people's instinctual need for spiritual love (SLove)—the selfless kind of love that falls at the highest level of human needs tree. However, we are mostly seeking ELove (deficiency love)—the selfish need to be loved by someone who solves our insecurities, too.

136. Love has become such a precious commodity, nowadays, because it can satisfy a large variety of personal needs and motives. Yet, while people seek love in hopes of sharing a spiritual experience with their soul mates, many of them are inherently incapable of giving love. They merely want to be loved to heal their insecurities and control their partners.

137. People have a mix of the following motives for expressing or expecting love: (See the details in Appendix 3-A at the end of this chapter.)

- To *communicate* with their partners.
- To express their basic *feelings*.
- To release *psychological* pressures.
- To mimic their *spiritual* needs.
- To *control* their partners.
- To *manipulate* (abuse) their partners.

138. Accordingly, people's need for control, possessiveness, and jealousy are not the reflections of their true love. They only represent a person's rampant emotions and urge to control others for ELove, money, friendship, sex, etc.

139. Many people do not have the patience or time even for a simple friendship, yet insist on having a 'love' relationship. They disregard the primary principles, including respect and courtesy, to allow their friendship develop in a natural way. Instead, they depend on their weird games to incite a phony love. Therefore, the question is, 'How can people trust each other for a serious relationship if they do not even know how to be good friends?'

140. The main feature of successful friendships, which is missing in relationships, is that friends' limited expectations grow

naturally, without pressure or demand. Then, even if those expectations are not fulfilled, they usually do not argue or fight, but rather moderate their own expectations to sustain their friendship.

141. Overall, the meaning of the word 'love' has become too ambiguous and arbitrary due to many facts explained in this book, including individuals' unique needs and perceptions about love.

142. On the other hand, since love has simply become the locus of relationships in modern societies, we must at least know what it is and understand its role in relationships.

143. In particular, to appreciate love and possibly enjoy it, we should remove the ambiguities surrounding our impression of it. Accordingly, the following definitions might further clarify some of our misperceptions about love.

144. The word 'love,' in the context used nowadays, consists of people's impression (and expression) of their 1) urges, 2) feelings, and 3) moods during their search for a companion.

145. Love **Urges** are mostly sexual, but also driven by loneliness, insecurity, need for belonging, etc.

146. The **Feelings** related to humans' search for a soul mate are numerous, including delight, elation, lust, possessiveness, jealousy, hatred, anger, and all other feelings that humans face while chasing any desire. A variety of feelings emerges during their love related affairs, success, or failure.

147. The **Moods** that emerge during humans' search for a mate entail: Attraction, Romance, and Attachment. They evolve from a mix of urges and feelings, but also by our conscious assessment of the person we feel attracted to.

148. **Attraction** is triggered by physical appeal, lust, but also our careful appraisal of a person's qualities and resources. Our instinctual criteria for selecting a mate, mostly for bearing a child with this person, often play their role, too.

149. **Romance** is our innate impression of SLove (devotion) and our calculating expressions of passion in order to lure in our

beloved. Therefore, again, we are using both our instinctual and logical assets to find a companion.

150. **Attachment** is the effect of closeness to an individual and enjoying the compassion satisfied by this union.

151. We have historically combined all these urges, feelings, and moods and called it love, thus creating a vague definition to deal with.

152. People suffer because of love for two main reasons: First, the forces behind their love urges, feelings, and moods are not clear to them in order to deal with the sources of their anxieties directly. Second, they assume love is a lasting condition.

153. Understanding the true meaning and implications of love might help us curb our initial unwarranted enthusiasm and prepare ourselves better for its heartbreaking consequences.

154. The *urges, moods, and feelings* in individuals related to 'finding a companion' should be studied as psychological reactions—symptoms of love—but not love itself.

155. True love is that one instinctual urge that we have identified as SLove. Love, in its purest sense, is just a simple, selfless appreciation for the mere 'being' of another person without having any selfish urges to own, control, or impose one's needs upon that person.

156. This pure feeling of SLove, engraved in our unconscious, is occasionally directed towards our beloved, too, but usually for a short period. This is because we usually have a hard time internalizing SLove until we learn to become a selfless individual.

157. We create all kinds of images and love moods (in the form of attraction and romance) in our minds when some flickers of SLove strike us. However, these love moods only reflect our urgent urges for 'sex' and 'compassion,' as we struggle to find a companion.

158. Overall, merely our fervent 'need for a companion' (once directed towards a particular person) creates all those urges,

feelings, and moods that we customarily (though wrongly) attribute to love.

159. This subtle understanding about love is important, because it makes us think and put our love related urges and feelings into a proper perspective. We remember that merely our 'need for a companion' and 'sense of loneliness' often make us behave in strange ways.

160. Furthermore, we should realize that the real cause of our restlessness and loneliness is not love (or a lack of it), even though we crave more love the lonelier we get. The real cause of our loneliness is our rising inability to *relate* to one another, while our obsession to find a soul mate keeps rising at the same time.

161. This awareness might goad us to adopt a new mentality: to either give less importance to having a companion, or go about finding him/her in a more honest, productive, and natural manner.

162. Our 'need for a *reliable* companion' is actually so impaired it has turned into '*desperation* for a companion,' nowadays.

163. Yet, we remain hopeful all our lives to find a soul mate who would fulfil most of our personal needs.

164. Realistically, however, our chances for finding a soul mate is remote, and then realizing companionship's 'potentialities' (and sustaining good relationships) has even a lower chance for all the reasons enumerated in this book.

165. Nowadays, partners can hardy fulfil even each other's basic need for sex on a long-term basis, let alone all those more complex needs for ELove, compassion, and SLove.

166. At the same time, people seem to have a chronic optimism about their relationships' potentialities despite their repeated failures, frustration, anger, and desperation.

167. Our desperation for a companion will keep rising, since we cannot sustain a relationship or trust our partners enough.

168. A major issue is that we have become too idealistic. Instead of understanding the roots of relationship problems and our

role in causing many of them, we keep dreaming about a soul mate and an ideal relationship with another partner. We do not see the futility of our search for love or a soul mate before revamping our own mentalities and personalities.

169. Naturally, the more relationships fail, the more desperate people get, which ironically only heightens their craving for love even more. It is easy to notice that the more a person is desperate to find a companion, the faster and deeper he/she falls in love.

170. In all, our obsession for love, nowadays, is a reflection of our loneliness and desperation for a companion. However, our exaggerated expectations (including love) destroy our relationships and we feel even more desperate and lonely. This vicious cycle is ruining people's trust in one another and their expressions of love.

171. If we just realize that love cannot be the success factor for relationships, we might decide to reassess and revamp our own personalities, lifestyles, needs, demands, and methods of going about finding a companion.

172. The way we have become—so haughty and oversensitive—is to be blamed for the failure of relationships, not the lack of love or couple's inabilities to be romantic.

173. **Attraction** has been a rather instinctual mood (process) for selecting a mate going back millions of years in the history of evolution. Nowadays, we get attracted, or pretend to be attracted, to someone based on many other factors, too, such as his/her wealth, social standing, ambition, appearance, etc. Thus, the purity of attraction is questionable, nowadays.

174. **Romance** has always existed in nature, too, yet its role has also been tentative (like 'Attraction') for both animals and humans. Still, we like to have lots of it, nowadays—a naive demand that is increasing expectations and clashes when couples cannot deliver romance naturally on a regular basis.

175. **Attachment** has evolved in humans, as the need for support to nurture their offspring emerged for our ancestors many

millenniums ago. It was mostly a temporary arrangement, too, then partners felt independent again, when children could live on their own.

176. Now, we have gotten used to the idea of having a long-term commitment with a partner. Aside from historical, religious, and ethical influence, this mentality has grown stronger as humans have become more insecure, calculating, and needy for love and compassion in recent history.

177. At the same time, we have become too arrogant, insecure, phony, and demanding, thus sabotage our chances to sustain long commitments with anybody.

178. Nonetheless, our yearning for both romance and attachment (including commitment) appears to be largely self-imposed moods. It reflects humans' insecurities as well as struggle for social morality.

179. Love has always been addressed as a combination of many feelings, urges, and moods related to humans' search for a companion. If the ancient Greek had defined ten different kinds of love, now psychologist come up with six or eight types again based on its symptoms.

180. However, dividing love into certain categories by attaching certain feelings to each category would not help the existing chaos in relationships. It only convolutes the meaning of a natural concept like love even more.

181. In the end, the essence of love is always that simple notion of selflessness towards another being regardless of all the feelings and urges that manifest in each particular case, e.g., love towards our children, parents, a person, or even objects, such as Nature, artistic passion, etc. Love is always the unique feeling of SLove regardless of all the emotions that get attached to it.

182. Sometimes, we make a big fuss about the way a lover feels restless, jealous, depressed, sleepless, etc. However, these symptoms are common in many other situations, too, when any special plan or desire of a person is threatened. People

lose sleep and become restless about any serious matter that occupies their minds, e.g., a project, a catastrophe, etc., or get jealous if a job promotion is given to another person.

183. The symptoms of love should not affect the nature of love, if it is true love. Even compassion, which is noble and often more precious than even love, should not be mixed up with love.

184. Pure, unselfish SLove satisfies some peaceful emotions and urges of humans, but it does not lead to self-destruction or war with our beloved. This is the simple definition of love adopted in this book.

185. Hatred and rage, when love fails, show that our perception of 'love' had not been pure (SLove). Obviously, many of our selfish and destructive urges and feelings influence our *impression and expression* of love. Thus, it helps to know the real motives behind these urges and feelings.

186. In all, people's sense of love, nowadays, consists of some kind of mixed urges for sex, compassion, and an impression of SLove. Then they express some feelings and moods, all in an attempt to find a companion.

187. Hormones that rule human urges do not seem to support people's excessive expectations from love and relationships, either. Discussions in Chapter Five about human hormones reveal many other facts.

188. In the past, love had little impact on people's daily lives and their relationships, simply because people did not read many books and were not exposed to such relentless amount of misleading propaganda about love. They had many real life hardships to worry about. They were not so obsessed about expressing themselves as much, either.

189. The new social values have brainwashed us to make love the locus of relationships, thus inflict enormous pressures upon ourselves and our partners.

190. Love has become confused with attraction and mixed up with many other human urges and feelings. The purposes of

love and relationships are also muddled in people's minds in a destructive way.

191. Overall, the destiny of love does not look bright because:

- The meaning of love has become ambiguous and useless, especially for building relationships. However, we like to make a big deal about the phrase "I love you." In effect, the use of the word love is too hypocritical considering people's varied purposes for, and understanding of, love.
- The general increase in social complexity, sexuality, and corruption makes people less trustful of one another and their expressions of love every day. At the same time, people insist that relationships and love must be built on absolute trust and honesty.

192. Our limited options to face the reality of relationships and love are to:

- Become selfless and internalize SLove,
- Pursue love affairs here and there if we are lucky,
- Live alone while waiting for love,
- Use MLove to instil mutual respect and civility in our relationships.

193. Using MLove in relationships has other advantages, too: It provides a venue for partners to be romantic without raising relationship expectations or stirring misunderstandings about their love expressions.

194. Another merit of MLove is that expressing one's feelings through MLove would partially respond to partners' need for SLove.

195. MLove also fulfils some of partners' ELove needs. This happens since people's *subconscious* can easily substitute MLove for ELove, while their *conscious* minds remember the subtle intentions of MLove.

196. MLove is a voluntary and possibly periodical gesture by one or both partners. A partner should not turn that into an

expectation; otherwise, it would be ELove and not MLove anymore.

197. Obviously, the word 'love' covers a big variety of meanings and none of them actually reflects true love (SLove). This ambiguity and misperception in people's minds cause so much conflict in relationships.

198. Furthermore, 'love' is perceived and applied differently by people according to their psychological and circumstantial needs.

199. In all, love has no uniform implications to draw upon or set expectations for. We can use it arbitrarily only to soothe our need for compassion without making an issue out of it or expecting long-term commitment on that basis. "You said you loved me!" is a common complaint when couples try to interpret 'love' according to their vague perceptions.

200. Accordingly, couples get hurt a lot due to their erroneous impressions of love, and because they annoy each other with their exaggerated expectations for love and attention.

201. Couples destroy not only their chances for building peaceful relationships, but also the opportunity of understanding the meaning of SLove.

202. Accordingly, expecting love in relationships or hoping to find happiness through love is a fantasy in general, although a few people can attain all that in certain circumstances, mostly through self-awareness and being a better person themselves.

203. Our culture permeates many invalid myths about love. We believe that:

- Love is the test of success for relationships.
- Love lasts forever.
- Love makes a relationship last forever.
- Relationships must be validated by love.
- Relationships thrive on love.
- Anybody considering a serious relationship should and would find a person to exchange love with each other.

- Expressing love regularly ensures relationships' success.
- Love is a common phenomenon that everyone grasps and is capable of delivering.
- Love is a common commodity that everyone must find and enjoy in his/her life.
- When there is love, relationship problems are rare and manageable.
- Love overcomes all the relationship problems.
- Partners have control over their feelings to love each other forever.

204. The above myths are useless and furthest from the nature of relationships in the new era. Love does not have the power or meaning stipulated in those myths. Nor do relationships necessarily last longer if partners start their relationships with love.

205. We are not learning any lesson from the fact that almost all relationships in the modern world have started based on *some kind of love* and they still keep failing miserably. It is amazing.

206. Couples have become both too romantic and antagonistic, nowadays.

207. Many couples are frustrated and confused, as they feel trapped in their loveless (maybe hostile) relationships. This is especially stressful for those who are adamant about love being the essence of relationships.

208. Hypocrisy and deceit overwhelm our relationships and love affairs when we constantly draw on Model to play games and manipulate our partners.

209. Being natural requires keeping Model at the minimum level needed only for etiquette and tactfulness, before it leads to phoniness. Accordingly, using MLove in our relationships must be sincere and natural to help couples relate fairly and exchange compassion.

210. A simple fact about the meaning of love has been ignored in our new culture: We do not appreciate that the more one seeks SLove, the more one must be honest and sincere in character. Yet, people have lost their ability to be natural and sincere because of all the complex games that have been introduced in relationships in recent decades.
211. Like other aspects of social life these days, a superficial (embellished) love is encouraged and preferred to sincerity and reality.
212. Even 'love' is contaminated by pervasive selfishness and gross misperceptions, nowadays.
213. Partners look for unconditional (selfless) love from each other, but impose many conditions to ensure *equality,* even in terms of the level of love they exchange.
214. While equality, in the sense of *fairness,* is the foundation of democratic societies, the concept of equality has turned into a socio-political platform to further spread our demented social values.
215. The concept of love is ordinarily confused in the minds of couples who not only make the equality of love a primary relationship requirement, but also *retaliate* harshly when their love is not returned equally.
216. We imagine that we can hide our insincerity, mistrust, and dishonesty from the rest of the world forever. However, this mentality only shows our arrogance and high trust in Model to bail us out. The good news is that people can detect each other's true nature, despite all the elaborate games they play to pretend a false personality of themselves and to conceal their calculating nature.
217. The games and retaliation schemes in relationships show how absurd the idea of measuring our relationships' strength by 'love' is. We just ignore all these contradictions and keep seeking SLove in such a contaminated, phony environment.
218. Loving someone requires a special talent, knowledge, and awareness.

219. For true love, partners need a highly developed character. For example, only a fool might believe in love expressions by a naïve person.
220. The complexity of both love and relationships is evident in the way couples use Ego, Mode, and Self, to communicate their perceived feelings of love.
221. Since love is the glue holding couples together nowadays, other aspects of their relationships become hard to manage and appreciate, too, when love begins to lose its intensity.
222. Promises and wedding vows actually create many problems of their own in relationships. For one thing, promises raise partners' expectations from each other unrealistically. The main issue, however, is that partners get a wrong impression regarding the security and permanence of their relationship. They set their expectation high and erroneously. They ignore that all relationships are vastly vulnerable and need constant attention and work to survive one more day.
223. Partners must monitor their relationship's health constantly and elude alienation by using 'Alienation Preparedness' methods, as explained in this author's book, *Marriage and Divorce Hardships.*
224. What we call love in our relationships is usually only a mix of lust, possessiveness, and psychological insecurities we have compiled through social interactions in line with our genetics. In fact, not even SLove (selfless love) is a success factor for relationships necessarily.

Appendix 3-A

Motives (Personal Needs) behind Love

We exchange love (mostly ELove) to satisfy many personal needs and motives. Some of these prominent motives are:

- To *communicate* with our partners. Showing passion may be only a means of striking a conversation with our partners for many reasons, maybe for measuring some aspects of the relationship, or possibly even for manipulating our partners.
- To express our basic *feelings*. We may express love to draw our partners' attention to our urgent feelings and needs. We might feel happy, fulfilled, depressed, lonely, lost, etc. We like to share any kind of feelings with our partners and hope to receive their sympathy, too.
- To release *psychological* pressures. We show passion to fulfil our needs for acceptance and dependence. Insecurity and need for continuous recognition motivate a partner to use ELove as a mechanism to enforce his/her dependency on his/her partner.
- To mimic our *spiritual* needs. We have an instinctual urge for SLove. Although our medium range needs prevent us from acting on this high-level need, SLove is triggered now and then subconsciously, e.g., when we hear a romantic tune or watch a drama. For a moment, we get in touch with this obscure feeling, i.e., SLove. We may eventually act upon it, but usually these spiritual experiences are fleeting moments that we cannot internalize and apply regularly. As noted before, SLove erupts only after fulfilling (or curbing) our basic and medium needs and becoming a needless and selfless person. This spiritual love requires these high levels of maturity and enlightenment.
- To *control* our partners. An inconspicuous, but common, purpose of love is to satisfy one's need for control. That is,

often, a person's urge for love is for controlling his/her partner somewhat easier. People exchange love phrases, hoping to enhance their partners' love for them, so that they can live within certain boundaries agreeable to one or both partners, depending on who loves the other more and who is setting the boundaries. People's rising urge for control is not always out of malice. They do it because that is the only method they know for managing their relationships and for prolonging them. Another reason for partners' 'need for control' is that they trust each other less every day, thus get an urge to impose controls on each other.

- To *manipulate (abuse)* our partners. Sometimes, a partner expresses love or attachment only for (ab)using his/her partner—mostly for his/her personal financial and sexual needs—with the least amount of sincerity in his/her words or attitude.

Chapter Four

Facts about

Personal Needs

The topic of personal needs is too vast and complex. Still, the impacts of personal needs on relationships are discussed generally with an emphasis on personal needs for dependence and independence at the end of the chapter due to their major roles in marriages. In all, the following facts reveal the nature of our personal needs related to relationships, the problems they cause, and the ways we can mitigate their negative effects on our relationships.

225. Our personal needs have increased exponentially in recent decades due to our growing misperceptions about love and happiness, the influence of consumerism, and our urges to imitate other people and the symbols of modernity. Our dire misperceptions and drive for pampering our rampant needs have raised our personal expectations from life and ruined our relationships, too.
226. Overall, modern people have become too needy for things, passion, and compassion. This epidemic merely reflects our insecurities and accelerating artificial needs that we have imposed upon ourselves by habit and imitation in modern societies.

227. Accordingly, our excessive personal needs have become too complex as well, because the authentic and artificial ones have been blending and creating new interpretations and expectations beyond our apprehension and ability to fulfil. Yet, we must somehow learn to deal with all these needs—both authentic and artificial ones—mostly by lowering their importance for our welfare. That is the only way to manage our lives and survive in relationships.

228. For one thing, we should remember that our personal needs are developed and triggered by a wide range of inner and outer forces. *Outer forces* refer to socioeconomic factors, upbringing, etc. These outer forces affect our perceptions of reality and we become too needy when we let social norms and propagandas control our brains.

229. On the other hand, *inner forces* comprise of:

- Instincts
- Genetics
- Habits (conditioning)
- Reactions (impulses)

230. Inner forces mainly constitute both our inherent or absorbed characteristics. We hardly have any control over these traits.. However, we can learn to monitor and manage them more effectively.

231. As we learn about the inner forces driving our minds and actions, our self-awareness and the quality of our lives would improve, while we also learn to reduce our neediness and overcome our misperceptions.

232. Furthermore, our self-awareness and knowledge of inner forces can help us bring objectivity into our relationships. For one thing, couples can learn that some *forces* beyond people's control develop and infect so much of their own and their partners' personalities and substandard attitudes.

233. It is also important to learn about the wide range and nature of personal needs and the ways they interact and affect us.

234. Overall, humans are driven by a set of progressive needs. Basic needs, such as food and shelter, are at the bottom of this 'personal needs tree'. Our needs for social interaction and recognition stand in the middle. Humans' higher needs consist of self-esteem and actualization. According to this theory, people climb up the 'needs tree' only as their lower needs are satisfied.

235. We usually have big difficulty satisfying our middle range needs, including relationships and recognition. Then, we rarely find the opportunity to strive for our higher needs. Our obsessions with our middle range needs hinder our chances to attend to the higher ones.

236. In particular, our lasting struggle to find and keep a suitable companion proves too frustrating and time-consuming. Yet, despite our relentless efforts, this need (for a companion) remains substantially unfulfilled for most of us.

237. Accordingly, we lose our chances to spend enough time to understand and work on our other personal or social needs. In particular, our needs for self-actualization, individualism, and spirituality remain unfulfilled. Therefore, we never learn to become a selfless and self-reliant person and realize the joy and tranquility of contentment.

238. Meanwhile, we have now grown an erroneous mentality and naively assume that relationships can magically fulfil our most prominent personal needs.

239. We also assume that relationships can somehow handle all the quirks that partners bring with them to this environment.

240. In reality, however, relationships only place more demands on partners and exacerbate their idiosyncrasies.

241. Instead of satisfying our personal needs, relationships cause more frustrations for couples, in fact, by limiting their time, energy, and opportunities for achieving their personal goals individually.

242. Expecting relationships to serve a vast variety of our raw obsessions is even a more naïve and egotistical attitude.

243. We assume our partners can (and should) respond to our varied personal needs, which we also selfishly believe are sensible.

244. We also imagine our partners are psychologically equipped to respond to our particular needs (such as compassion and love) at the exact time and manner we desire.

245. Overall, we assume that our partners are capable of making us happy. Couples make this common mistake when they start a relationship.

246. Therefore, contrary to our naïve presumptions, our personal needs usually get frustrated, instead of fulfilled, when we start a relationship.

247. Couples also ignore that, for improving their relationships, they should mostly recognize and adjust their own personal needs and expectations, instead of demanding their partners to change their attitudes.

248. In fact, we must find ways of fulfilling our personal needs (e.g., finding happiness) independently so that the burden on relationships is reduced.

249. It is depressing to see that finding a suitable companion has become such a challenging and frustrating endeavour in spite of the increasing number of matchmaking services and meeting places.

250. Sadly, nobody knows the relationships' generic needs and demands, nowadays, and how to fulfil them. Instead, people strive to focus on and fulfil their demented personal needs.

251. Couples also fail since no realistic definition of 'relationship needs' exists to prepare them for companionship challenges in the new era amidst so many other daily life demands. 'Relationship Needs' is elaborated in Chapter Eight.

252. Couples' lack of knowledge about relationships' specific needs has made them lose their sense of objectivity, thus many relationships get into trouble quickly, nowadays.

253. Instead, people assume relationships can fulfil their personal needs or empower them to do so personally. Yet, soon they

find their relationships an additional hindrance for achieving their personal goals. Every spouse gets frustrated because:

- Fulfilling even his/her basic needs, including sex, is now suddenly at the mercy of someone else.
- The cost of satisfying his/her needs feels too high and humiliating, against his/her convictions, integrity, and sense of independence. The cost mostly entails some type of compromise he/she must bear to oblige one's partner.
- He/she cannot seek relief anywhere else because of his/her commitment to their relationship. For example, if he/she seeks sex outside of their failing relationship, he/she faces the charge of adultery. It would be a taboo to satisfy a strong natural urge, a basic need that he/she could fulfil almost at will prior to entering a relationship.
- The situation spins out of control, since his/her partner's unending demands are unrealistic and it is not easy to abandon the relationship, either. The relationship stays in a stalemate indefinitely.

254. Furthermore, the atmosphere for personal need fulfilment is not calm and logical, nowadays. People get frustrated when their imaginary needs are not satisfied readily.

255. In fact, we witness people's hysteria for not succeeding to climb up the personal needs tree quickly enough and fulfil their ambitions, achieve happiness, or even find a somewhat perfect companion.

256. Thus, only by learning about the nature and authenticity of our personal needs and motivations behind them—mainly through self-awareness—we can also develop and boost our relationships.

257. In fact, the only way couples can build their relationships is for each partner to follow a serious regimen of self-analysis, develop his/her awareness about the complexity of human needs and behaviour in general, and learn how partners' idiosyncrasies infect their relationships.

258. Our biggest misperception is that our partners are in control of their personalities. We forget that both inner and outer forces largely cripple people mentally to control their Egos and logic.

259. As a symbol of civilization, we have developed laws, ethics, and etiquettes, since we believe people's urges and actions are often fuelled by erratic forces beyond their control. Yet, in our regular relationships, we keep ignoring this basic fact about humans' inherent inability to be good or reliable.

260. We have little patience for imperfections, as we arrogantly assume we are perfect ourselves. Furthermore, we expect others to be perfect, too, based on our perceived definition of perfection. These two misleading presumptions reflect the influence of our inner forces dictating our judgments and dulling our objectivity.

261. We seek a companion to satisfy three major personal needs: Sex, compassion, and love. These needs are the three pillars of relationships.

262. In the present frustrating environment, partners' needs for sex and compassion are jeopardized and they face mental and physical hardship. Those who insist on finding 'love' in a relationship, too, are in an even tougher position, as their expectations are beyond the limits of a normal relationship to begin with.

263. Yet, often, neither partner is at fault in these situations. They are both victims of their *complex needs* and rooted idiosyncrasies. They have been conditioned in society to set high expectations for their relationships. 'Complex needs' is meant here to reflect both our instinctual needs, such as sex, and those artificial ones, such as need for more things and more compassion. After all, these artificial needs are the symptoms of new lifestyles in modern society and we are helplessly obsessed by them.

264. Even partners' raw retaliations, when their complex needs remain unfulfilled, might be deemed natural if we see them

as defence mechanisms. As discussed in the future chapters, partners' varied quirks force them to react irrationally. To them, reacting or retaliating is their only tool to survive in this chaotic society. Their only guilt is their naive belief that they would get their needs satisfied faster in a relationship. They have naively disregarded the fact that their partners are entering relationships with many urgent needs and demands of their own with little interest, time, or patience to address other people's needs.

265. In addition, couples naively believe that they can convince their partners better through retaliation or by playing games. Often, actually, retaliation and playing games are all they know for controlling their relationships and partners.

266. Most relationships would have been considered acceptable if couples were not misled by their superficial needs. For example, partners believe that they deserve high attention from their companions and must actually be 'spoiled' by them rather regularly. Or as they get old, they mostly see the aging of their partner and not their own. Therefore, they try to revive their youthful memories with another person who is not so old and cranky like their spouses, and flatters them regularly, too.

267. That is, people's seeming urgent needs, e.g., sexuality and youthful adventures, usually make them lose sight of their longer-term needs that often restrict their pleasures.

268. A strong inner conflict burdens us all our lives, as our two fundamental needs for dependence and independence keep competing and clashing constantly in our minds.

269. In fact, all our needs are often at the mercy of our needs for dependence and independence. Our other needs (even our basic need for food) are boosted or dampened by our potent need for independence (or dependence) regardless of the consequences.

270. As we go through life, the number of our dependencies keeps rising, while we keep struggling to build our unique

identity and independence. We get frustrated often when our independence is jeopardized by our need for dependence on other people and society.

271. We hate the way our partner is squashing our independence. However, we also hate that we cannot depend on them enough. Accordingly, the level of our inner conflict due to our needs for dependence and independence keeps rising and straining our relationships.

272. Especially, with the added emphasis on individualism and independence in modern societies, both marital and personal conflicts due to couples' basic needs for both dependence and independence have become too prominent and more widespread in society. As a result, our inner conflicts have skyrocketed, too.

273. Creating and maintaining a balance between our conflicting needs for both independence and dependence is a tough job, even if we assume such a balance can be found.

274. In general, independence requires (and leads to) a great deal of isolation and self-reliance. Conversely, dependence is mostly synonymous with (need for) compassion.

275. Our partners and society in general do not know how to cope with our need for dependence. Often, they actually ridicule and take advantage of our perceived weakness, i.e. our inability to be independent.

276. Our inner conflicts actually heighten when we try to pretend to be more independent than we really feel we are, or can handle.

277. By exaggerating our need for independence (individualism), we are actually imposing another set of conflicting, artificial expectations on ourselves, which are unachievable.

278. At the same time, we are jeopardizing our chances to fulfil our need for dependence by alienating our partners through our exaggerated display of independence. These superficial needs and demands stir more inner conflicts for each partner as well as more clashes between partners.

279. Partners become aggressive in order to appear assertive, mostly because they do not know about, or cannot master, the delicate art of assertiveness for fulfilling their needs.
280. The artificial need to *show off* our independence, as a sign of freedom and identity, has become counterproductive for both our individualism and relationships.
281. The bottomline is that partners' need for dependence is now undervalued at so many levels by modern lifestyles, values, personal neediness, and social pressures. It is trendier to demonstrate one's aptitude for individualism. Thus, people pretend to be independent in order to fit and survive.
282. At the same time, the smart thing, nowadays, is to not rely on others or their words. They simply cannot deliver due to the limitations in their own lives and personalities, and not necessarily out of malice.
283. Meanwhile, there is an ongoing struggle between partners to maintain a balance of power, mostly through intimidations and games, merely to stop each other from dominating their relationship.
284. Everybody likes more independence for themselves but less for their partners.
285. With freedom (and independence), most people are mainly thinking about freedom to explore sexuality and love, and to be adventurous or reckless. This is an automatic reaction to our philosophy about life being short and living only once.
286. Couples' struggle to cope with their needs for dependence and independence has led to a bizarre development: Some couples seek separation with the slightest inconvenience in their relationships; and some couples accept adultery and abuse, because they are too apprehensive about loneliness and isolation. These prevalent extremes show the extent of value changes in new societies.
287. Overall, we are not as strong individuals as we pretend to be in our exaggerated show of independence and individuality.

288. We are not equipped and strong enough, either, to create a practical balance between our needs for independence and dependence in our relationships.

289. The desire for wealth and power has ruined our capacity to grasp our very basic need for true independence unselfishly, to free ourselves from people and symbols that constrict our ability to think straight. We pretend to be independent and free, but these gestures are usually too far from reality (our daily routines) and how we really feel.

The contentious issues about our needs for independence and dependence are summarized in the remainder of this chapter:

290. We are not quite conscious of our conflicting needs for both dependence and independence. Nor are we aware of the high repercussions of this conflict for us, our relationships, and society in general.

291. We do not know how to define or judge our personal needs for independence and dependence. We do not know how to be independent or dependent when we go about satisfying these needs alternately on a regular basis. Some pretend to be independent and needless when deep down their need for dependence is overwhelming. And some people damage their identities when they become submissive.

292. We play the kind of roles that society and people suggest, usually with the highest emphasis on independence, since we do not know how to set and maintain a practical balance between our needs for independence and dependence. Yet, everybody has a different balance of needs for dependence and independence according to his/her unique personality. Ignoring those needs and sticking to some fake balance (and role-playing through Model) raises our confusion and stress.

293. Couples do not know how to discuss and match their needs for dependence and independence—mostly because it might require some kind of compromise, which would be against

their presumed identities and independence. Therefore, they end up arguing about every detail or decision required for running their relationships.

294. Without knowing about our needs for independence and dependence and the balance most suitable for us, we expect our partners to behave as if they did know what the right balance should be. For example, we expect them to respect our independence when we suddenly feel it is time for us to be independent; we ask for a vaster boundary. Then, later, we expect them to be compassionate and attentive as soon as we need them to satisfy our dependence (ELove) mania.

295. We turn off our partners with our exaggerated expressions of independence. And we confuse them and ourselves with our foolish roles and games to enforce our alternating needs for independence and dependence. This confusing attitude makes it hard for partners to relate to each other.

296. Meanwhile, power struggles to dominate our partners, and enforce our gender identities, delay the matter of aligning our needs for dependence and independence. Just arrogance and phoniness prevail in this kind of environment. All these conditions hinder the task of bringing objectivity and peace into our marriages. Choosing a proper relationship model becomes very difficult, too.

297. As social complexity and the public's intelligence increase every year, people's demands for both independence and dependence will rise.

298. They seek more independence because society pushes them to express themselves and establish (prove) their identities, more explicitly. However, they also seek more dependence (need for a compassionate companion) because of the rising level of stress in their daily lives and the overall sense of loneliness. Therefore, people struggle more every day with their anxiety and inner conflicts, instead of aligning their needs for dependence and independence.

299. The topics covered in this book show how the imbalance (between our needs for independence and dependence) is forced upon us due to our lifestyles and mentalities.

300. Accordingly, relationships will become more instable in the future and their longevity will continue to decline.

301. Considering this inevitable prospect, it is crucial to ponder relationship facts, trends, and choices reiterated in this book very carefully, especially in terms of the 'radical changes,' suggested in Part III.

302. A side comment worth making, based on the above points, is that both our basic need for sex (including the urge for reproduction, especially for women) and our high-level need for selfless, spiritual love are instinctual needs. Thus, it appears that we have created most of the medium-range personal needs through evolution and according to cultural conditions. As we have felt psychologically weaker and more vulnerable within new environments, we have built all types of superficial needs to soothe our suffering and to deal with our dependencies on others. We have also introduced new social values and personal games to satisfy our urgent need for a companion, but also as part of couples' growing power struggles in relationships.

303. The above facts provide solid clues about the faltering state of relationships. They show that the faster our societies grow, i) the more superficial needs we impose on ourselves and our relationships, ii) the more complex the relationship environment gets, iii) the faster couples' inner conflicts rise, iv) the more people suffer because of relationships and a sense of loneliness, and, v) the more relationships fail.

304. As social values and couples' personal needs change during the course of history, the meaning, objectives, and format of their relationships change. Thus, they should be reassessed and redefined every few decades as well.

Chapter Five

Facts about

Hormones and Gender Differences

Gender differences and hormones are two other factors causing severe relationship conflicts and reducing partners' abilities to connect. This chapter discusses only a few primary facts about gender differences, hormones, and their offshoots in relationships. Chapter Eleven offers another hundred social and relationship trends caused by gender differences. Another book in this series is planned to discuss these sensitive topics exclusively in more detail. It is easy to imagine the immense side effects of hormones and gender differences way beyond everything already listed in this book.

With regard to human hormones, scientists have reached the following conclusions:

305. Sexual activity stirs the mood for cuddling and attachment, but too much sex usually erodes the sense of attachment.
306. Although attachment raises sexual urge initially, prolonged attachment might eventually dampen the urge for sex.
307. Romance and attachment are not proven to be related.
308. Attachment might erode romance.
309. Romance might subdue sexual urges.

310. Humans are not naturally built to be monogamous, unlike some animals that have the right chemistry for it.
311. The immense sense of passion often dies within six months to about two years.
312. Humans are chemically (instinctually) inclined to connect to different people for satisfying different urges (romance, sex, attachment).
313. The effects of hormones and mood changes, especially for women during pregnancy, childbirth, menstrual cycle, and menopause, make gender differences and conflicts even more prominent.

In terms of gender differences due to hormonal, conditional, or other factors, the following points are observed:

314. While both genders have equal sexual drives, they often have different motives for acting upon it.
315. Women's natural superiority in creating and safeguarding their offspring appears to contribute to the fact that men lose their priority in relationships when children are born. This reality leads to a variety of misperceptions, inner conflicts, and frictions in relationships.
316. Another outer force jeopardizing relationships, nowadays, without anyone's fault is that women are in a hasty process of transition in terms of the progressive role they would like to play in society and relationships.
317. Women's new role in relationships is not understood even by most women, let alone by men who are expected to not only know what the new format should be, but also respond positively, too.
318. A special situation seems to have emerged: Due to men's passivity, women find it necessary to become aggressive in order to attain the assertiveness they need urgently.
319. It would be an inherently difficult task, for men especially, to attain the changes required in terms of gender roles, even

in a timelier manner, even if they agreed to the changes women are asking.

320. Within this confusing and stressful situation, all kinds of vain aggressions by both men and women are convoluting the transition process. Instead of progress, we witness more sabotage, retaliation, games, divorces, family murders, and suicides.

321. The bottomline is that men have now lost their identity (whatever it was, good or bad) and do not understand the sensibility of what is expected of them. And women are frustrated, too, because they cannot prove and enforce a new identity, which they believe they know what it is.

322. The result of the current confusion (about gender identities) is that partners get fed up with their struggles to convince each other logically. Therefore, they try to dominate each other or resort to divorce.

323. What works for women in a relationship does not work for men anymore, and vice versa. Especially, men and women mistrust the opposite genders much more than their own. The rising same-sex relationships *might be* partly because partners get along better.

324. It appears that we are reaching an era where men can no longer be what women want (in terms of character) and vice versa.

325. In all, both genders are going through a painful, confusing transition period.

326. The transition period mainly refers to the process of men and women learning their relationship roles in the new era. However, in reality, it refers to the long period for couples, especially women, to appreciate that their expectations from relationships are not logical and feasible.

327. People, especially women, are too idealistic, ambitious, neurotic, and stressed out, nowadays, due to their new roles, lifestyles and fantasies.

328. Women fuss a lot about their need for independence, but also demand to be spoiled. Ironically, they do not see the conflict, either.

329. Many people, especially women, take the flattery they get too seriously, as a sign of their opportunities to find a better mate once they leave their spouses. Then, after separation, they realize how they have been misled.

330. People, especially men, are enjoying the present situation with multiple dating and all, while they (mostly women) are getting more frustrated due to their failure to find a qualified partner and also facing their mates' (mostly men's) rising passivity.

331. Men and women are so incompatible in general that when, by chance, they match and love one another truly for a long time, it seems like a magical and spiritual sensation beyond our normal (expected) worldly experiences. It is such a revelation and coincidence. Still we naïvely believe love should happen to all of us, thus we seek it obsessively like a reasonable expectation.

332. The increasing rivalry and clashes between men and women look like some kind of all out gender warfare. The level of insults, belittling, retaliations, intimidations, manipulations, abuses, badmouthing, power struggles, crying, making a scene, competitions, screaming, blackmailing, and playing games to outsmart one another, just keep increasing.

333. Men and women are becoming increasingly alienated due to the changing social values and couples' drive to establish their gender identities better (often at the cost of weakening the other gender's identity). It appears that inherent gender differences are also adding fuel to the rising couples' pains and alienation in relationships.

334. Many of the clashes between men and women are due to women's higher instinctual tendency challenging men's higher logical predisposition.

335. In reality, however, both our instincts and logic are usually flawed, anyway. Therefore, often, nobody is right due to his or her erroneous perceptions and lack of objectivity.

336. Then problems increase because men and women want to change each other's decision processes, i.e., to make them more logical or intuitive—more like themselves. They fail because the instinctual tendencies of women and the logical urges of men are too deep-rooted to change quickly even if they realized the need for it. Their inherent personality traits often hinder this change to happen.

337. Women have a harder time in satisfying their conflicting needs for dependence and independence than men do. This is due to women's emphasis, nowadays, on independence as a means of affirming their identity. This pressure aggravates their conflicting (instinctual) urges for both dependence and independence.

338. Instinctually, women seek security and dependence more than men do. For example, women are more eager to find love and a social partner, because they not only are more optimistic about the possibility of finding their soul mates, but also crave love harder instinctually—due to their higher urges for reproduction, socializing, and social adaptation (Model). In addition, their exaggerated show of, and search for, independence hinders the natural fulfilment of their need for dependence. Accordingly, the more independence they acquire, the more they feel deprived of satisfying their urge for dependence.

339. Therefore, women are facing a big dilemma, nowadays: On the one hand, they like to depend on men, for procreation and for fulfilling their higher social needs due to their higher Model. On the other hand, they feel the urgency to assert their identity by proving their independence. This dilemma creates inner conflict and confusion for women and widens the gender gap, too. They usually do not admit or feel this inner conflict, but surely struggle with it subconsciously.

340. Seeking more independence is also a matter of 'life phase' for women. While raising and enjoying their kids, they feel empowered and independent due to their maternal power, but also because they presume their men are sticking around for emergencies, anyway. Once their kids are grown and gone, however, their need for dependence takes precedence again, especially if men have strayed.
341. Inherently, women need dependence on men for general support and completing their social identity, too, though they prefer to hide this fact.
342. Men's inner conflict in terms of dependence/independence is straightforward and simpler. They look for independence instinctually, but need to depend on women to fulfil some of their basic needs, including compassion and sex. They are helpless without women for managing their daily routines, while inherently they keep valuing their own independence highly.
343. Therefore, while both genders strive for both dependence and independence regularly, they do so for totally different reasons. Furthermore, they go through this cycle even more forcefully at different stages of their relationships as well. They start a relationship to fulfil their need for dependence (mostly their primary needs, e.g., sex and ELove). Soon, however, they take their relationship for granted and press for a complex need like independence (according to their naïve perceptions of, and unique needs for, independence.)

Many other points (over 100) about the implications of gender differences in relationships are discussed in Chapter Eleven where relationship trends are discussed. Those trends reflect gender's peculiar views about their relationships and the new ways they behave towards one another. Anyway, those trends are symptoms of the emerging or inherent gender differences that could have been listed in this chapter as new revelations (facts) in relationships.

Chapter Six
Facts about
Social Environment and Values

In recent decades, our relationships have shaped too closely around social environment and values, which only propagate superficiality and arrogance. Therefore, marital characteristics, nowadays, are not in line with humans' natural capacities and needs. Instead, we have created a shoddy social structure and relationship mishmash that is incapable to serve either humans or a civilized society. Especially, with women's evolving role in society and the waning of religions, we have grown many idiotic roles and demands in society and relationships. Social norms and values have become too pretentious and harmful, yet we are relying on these values to build our relationships and personal lives. These are all basic facts that need personal and social scrutiny for any possible improvements if we can revamp our mentalities and needs somewhat. Some other vital facts regarding the effects of social environment and values on relationships are explained in the following pages.

344. We no longer have a reliable culture to guide people in their choices and help them get along effectively. Instead, now we only pamper a society filled with vanity and conflicts.
345. People are getting more insecure due to society's crooked structure and values, thus they have become needier for love

and attention. When they do not get them at the desired level, they feel even more lost and lonely.

346. In return, people's rising desperation and lack of morality is not only ruining their lives, but also damaging the social structure and values more every day.

347. Relationships have become important, nowadays, because people's basic needs, e.g., food and shelter, are satisfied somewhat easier in modern societies. With relatively less pressing issues and hardships that most people around the world face daily, we luckier humans fuss too much about love and happiness, at the expense of losing our grasp of life and relationships' real needs.

348. Relationships appear like the best antidote for loneliness, too, because we cannot live independently anymore despite all our pretensions for individualism and freedom.

349. At the same time, providing constant attention to our cranky, insecure partners is a big responsibility that causes anxiety, besides all the extra work needed for running our careers, relationships, and other family affairs.

350. Furthermore, our accurate views of corruption and duplicity in society raise our cynicism about people's truthfulness and authenticity overall.

351. A big hurdle in relationships is that people trust one another less every day due to bad personal experiences and rampant socioeconomic corruption in modern societies.

352. On the other hand, the high percentage of marriage failures and ensuing headaches make relationships too risky these days. So absolute caution regarding the words and promises of our partners is warranted.

353. The cost (consequences) of trusting our partners is high now, because they usually disappoint us eventually. However, the cost of not showing full trust in them is also too high, as they find it insulting and a sign of our indifference towards them. These pervasive, dire dilemmas, plus couples' general cynicism, put extra pressure on couples and relationships.

354. Many humble individuals are out there who could be in good relationships together if they were not deterred by their (usually justified) paranoia regarding the current state of relationships and their lack of trust in people.
355. Mistrust is now a natural (and often necessary) condition in relationships. This is merely a consequence of social life and not a sign of a person's weakness or selfishness.
356. Eliminating or overcoming the rooted causes of mistrust in relationships is almost impossible, too, since they are just symptoms of new social structure that advocates arrogance, greed, individualism, and materialism.
357. However, people's mistrust is often also caused by their own oversensitivity and misperceptions, which then affects their behaviour and their partners' added mistrust in them. In all, partners must remain conscious of the high possibility and causes of misjudging each other.
358. We should not expect our partners to trust us completely, especially when we feel the difficulty of trusting them fully ourselves.
359. We can never know *who we are* or *who they are* and they can never know *who they are* or *who we are*. We should honour these two facts with open minds. We struggle all our lives to find ourselves and happiness, to no avail. So, how can we expect others to know us and trust us when even we do not? It is simply impossible to build trust based on our doubtful perceptions of ourselves and others.
360. We rather know that our primary (premarital) impressions of our partners are often untrue and incomplete. Therefore, our inherent mistrust is partly due to our wisdom about the high likelihood that the real character of a person usually manifests only after some, or years of, cohabitation.
361. Accordingly, we should not view love and trust as reliable factors for measuring relationships' health anymore. Sadly, these fanciful criteria are often misleading and illogical, nowadays, due to people's tainted mentalities in a society

filled with deceit. People often lie about their love or trust to avoid confrontations, or to be tactful and wise. Furthermore, demanding trust or love beyond people's natural capacity brings only more duplicity and phoniness into relationships.

362. Deep down, we know that couples' sentimental promises or commitments are not reliable. Especially, taking the phrase 'I love you' seriously, as a sign of commitment, is naïve.

363. We must come to terms with two major facts in the new era: 1) it is natural that partners lose trust in each other to some extent soon, and, 2) we should learn to live in relationships with imperfect trust levels, instead of making a big issue about it. We should be ultra cautious at the time of starting our relationships, but remain flexible about the inevitable mistrust and disappointments later on.

364. Of course, building this type of mentality is difficult. Thus, a progressive relationship framework and set of principles must be propagated in society gradually.

365. People do not know how to be tactful or observe even basic etiquettes and ethics, but keep insisting on the purity of their souls.

366. While everybody is obsessed about finding his/her soul mate, the chance of it ever happening is slim. However, we all have difficulty accepting this fact, since we want to stay positive and sociable. Our romantic search for a soul mate is hindering us from perceiving and building our relationships realistically.

367. Relationships also force lifestyle changes and adaptation, often for tolerating our partner's idiosyncrasies and fitting with our partners' family habits and conflicting preferences.

368. However, instead of learning about the means of adapting ourselves to new relationship environment, we still only try to push our outmoded mentalities and methods.

369. All along, we struggle and hope to change our partner to fit our needs and make our relationships prosper. Doggedly, we see no need for adjusting our own attitudes and values.

370. Hope is an innate urge that keeps us motivated in our boring lives, but it must not make us dogmatic, e.g., about finding love in our relationships or the possibility of making our partners change their attitudes. Hope is a rather useful urge for survival, but not a reliable decision factor.

371. Overall, people do not change unless they feel the need for it through years of meditation and self-awareness, mainly for personal goals and not somebody else's benefit, e.g., his/her spouse. Thus, partners' retaliations, games, and intimidations to change each other merely reflect their own naivety.

372. In our present convoluted environment, often partners end up ruining each other's lives, instead of enriching it. This is because life is getting more complex and stressful every year and people have harder times coping with social pressures, while they live longer, too. People are now too stressed and impatient to deal with their growing, excessive relationship demands effectively.

373. The longer partners stay in a relationship, the more potent and incompatible their conflicting needs for dependence and independence get. Accordingly, this imbalance raises both the level of personal inner conflicts and the pressure placed on their relationship.

374. The more complex our societies and interactions become, the more we feel a need to control the sources of potential threats to our physical and mental welfare, including our partners. This is especially true, since we trust people much less, nowadays, than we did even a few decades ago.

375. We never recognize the sources of our crooked behaviour, or we deny their destructive effects on our relationships. Yet, even if we accept our flaws, we can hardly do much about them easily, anyway.

376. Old scars and hurt feelings cannot be erased easily. Their deep effects can always be traced in one's damaged psyche and crude personality that often appear through one's abrupt aggression, self-pity, and spite.

377. External (outer) forces, e.g., Nature, society, economy, and work environments, influence our moods, reactions, and outlooks about life, people, and our relationships.

378. External forces turn into either *conditional* or *reactional* forces within each person.

379. Conditional forces are those personal habits and values that we have adopted wholeheartedly, like greed and arrogance. They are the absorbed effects of *external forces*.

380. Conditional forces severely influence couples' perceptions and priorities in relationships. And the chance of partners' compatibility becomes very remote when those conditional forces mix with couples' genetic eccentricities.

381. Conditional forces also entail our doubts, insecurities, and quirks.

382. Reactional forces (defence mechanisms), such as anger and retaliation, reside in our unconscious and subconscious minds, and then suddenly activate our nervous system with a strong blow.

383. Clearly, under the hostile relationships' settings, each one of us turns into another hurtful *external force* for our partners.

384. A great deal of anger and stress is out there in society due to people's inability to find a suitable companion or enjoy their existing relationships. Partners just keep arguing and blaming each other's lack of common sense to understand their seemingly justified needs or their responsibilities for their relationship's downfall.

385. At the same time, the rising level of stress in society has made us vulnerable and too needy for sympathy, but there is nobody out there to give it to us.

386. Couples' ability to give and receive compassion depends on how humble and enlightened they really are. However, this crucial quality is declining fast among humans.

387. As a practical step, partners should begin to realize that, nowadays, the sense of commitment is vastly eroded by people's growing need for individualism.

388. Our high expectations from life and positive thinking make us believe we can find (or could have found) a better partner than the one we have. We believe we deserve a better one and he/she can be found if we look for him/her. However, all seemingly desirable partners prove inadequate again soon enough.
389. Thus, for relative tranquility, we must finally learn the art of living rather independently with or without a partner, instead of seeking a soul mate to bring us happiness and security.
390. Nevertheless, we always face a major dilemma (trade off) in life: companionship stir headaches and tranquility demands loneliness and self-reliance. The question is how to choose the best option for us based on our personality.
391. Of course, the ultimate question is whether we can develop novel relationship models for the new era, to fit couples' personalities and provide an atmosphere for a rather tranquil family life. This author believes that this option is plausible if we build a relationship framework and its corresponding principles to bring objectivity back into relationships.
392. With the constant increase of relationship conflicts, only a proactive (preventative) approach might stop relationship breakdowns. Partners must foresee and prevent relationship conflicts as much as possible at a high conscious level.
393. Instead of depending on partners to imagine the purposes of relationships and behave randomly based on their fantastic interpretations, a workable framework suitable for current social conditions must be made available to everybody.
394. We need practical principles to gauge relationships' success objectively, instead of letting the selfishness and neediness of partners make this fundamental judgment. Presently, only partners' arrogance is being measured during their conflicts, instead of the health of their relationships.
395. Instead of relying on couples' or their in-laws' opinions, an objective set of modest criteria should define relationships' health and success. In this environment, 'relationships' is

viewed as an independent *entity* free from crude judgments and perceptions of partners.

396. As we insist on more independence and individualism, the need for teamwork and communication becomes greater for keeping our egos under a leash.

397. Of course, for teamwork, partners need genuine qualities, including modesty and objectivity. Yet, the rising obsession for individualism is hindering our chances for modesty.

398. Overall, we are placing a lot of pressure on society and our partners with our rampant needs for things, sympathy, and security. This attitude and approach is limiting the chances of relationships following a practical path.

399. Someday soon, we must realize and agree that relationship expectations set beyond some modest, humanistic levels are artificial and imposed by demented and deprived people. Then, we can come together to redefine relationships as an independent entity with unique needs.

400. The obvious first step for assessing relationship conflicts is to establish whether they are genuine or only the outcome of partners' exaggerated expectations, unfulfilled personal needs, or idiosyncrasies. Yet, the question is who would be doing this assessment for couples and society as a whole, and according to what yardsticks? Depending on marriage counsellors and scholars has so far failed to bring solutions.

401. The reality is that before any outsider, including a marriage counsellor, can be of any use, people must learn a variety of new principles about relationships and begin to adjust their mentalities about the purposes of relationships.

402. Too many relationships are ruined, nowadays, because of partners' subjective assessments and hasty decisions.

403. A simple fact is that the rising complexity of relationships cannot be handled loosely anymore. It would be too risky to depend on erratic perceptions and interpretations of people to define relationships randomly. We need a rather universal relationship framework.

404. Out of necessity, everybody would realize eventually that marital decisions must become less arbitrary and emotional.

405. Clearly, couples' unique personalities lead to a vast variety of relationship types. Yet, following a progressive universal framework would maximize relationships' effectiveness for everybody with varied deformities. Trusting some generally acceptable principles for gauging our relationships would be preferable to relying on our subjective (and often deceptive) views about our relationships' rationality and health. This basic tool can minimize relationship conflicts

406. The deep sense of failure to find our soul mates, despite our lifelong search and struggles, causes us lasting psychological scars and stress.

407. Experts suggest many kinds of solutions for relationship problems and still relationships keep failing more than ever. This indicates that none of those solutions really works. The mere fact that there are so many incongruent solutions (all these variations) reflects that counsellors have not been able to build uniform and dependable solutions. The main reason is that no fix platform for relationships exists.

408. We must realize that the present solutions and simpler books that focus on quick fixes cannot help people. It is like building a house without a foundation.

409. Therefore, our ultimate objective, as individuals, society, and government should be to bring objectivity back into our relationships by developing and advocating a progressive relationship framework and a set of relationship principles.

410. The matters of love and relationships in modern societies are more complex than the laws of physics, because they hardly submit to any logic or formula.

411. The worst kind of therapy is when couples are encouraged to play phony roles to express passion or compassion as a mechanism for saving their relationships. Role-playing is obviously an artificial activity that usually induce more frustration in the end if partners are not intellectually (and

emotionally) convinced about the authenticity of their own (or their partner's) feelings and words.

412. People's inabilities to express their feelings are often not due to a lack of communication skill. Usually, the problem lies deep in people's psyches and remains beyond repair.

413. It is time for a more comprehensive approach to study the nature of relationship problems. We must study the needs of the modern world and scrutinize all the emerging facts.

414. We must study *what* has changed in society, *how* they are affecting relationships, and *why* radical changes are needed.

415. We must admit that our perceptions of reality (and society) is severely damaged, nowadays, as we have introduced more artificial needs in our lives, and because we have been propagating many shallow jargons about the meaning of life and happiness. Therefore, our challenge must be to develop relationship principles that fit modern relationships.

416. The major assumption for couples must be that the chance of their relationship failing is much higher than succeeding.

417. Accordingly, couples need some kind of guidelines urgently and personal wisdom to make their relationships last.

418. Most importantly, we should plan and behave according to the statistics and experiences around us. They all indicate that *marriage is a temporary arrangement* unless a miracle makes it last as long as we hope it should.

419. On the other hand, this raised awareness might motivate us indeed to make realistic efforts and save our relationships. Our new mentality to envision relationships as a temporary arrangement can actually help couples make it last longer.

420. We must reconsider our views of relationships, redefine our expectations sensibly, and be ready for the worst scenario, i.e., separation.

421. Why partners wait until they hate each other so much they cannot even look into each other's eyes? Why not separate civilly as soon as they realize they cannot relate realistically and remember that in most cases people cannot change?

422. Following our present approach would only make finding a companion harder due to, i) couples' excessive expectations from relationships, ii) their rising mistrust, iii) occupational stress, and, iv) the complexity and ambiguity of values in modern societies.

423. At the same time, the first sign of disagreement, nowadays, leads to partners' power struggles to set their territories and inform each other of their urgent personal needs.

424. Partners' urge for assertiveness engages them in all kinds of destructive schemes, supposedly to make their relationship work. They play games and resort to retaliation even when their intentions might be unselfish.

425. They do so because they do not know of any better method to curb their frustration and deal with relationship conflicts that keep growing every day. They often play these games merely for the sake of forcing a solution. They sincerely feel they are helping their partner and their relationship.

426. However, these games and retaliations often end in disaster. Even some civilized games, such as a partner's temporary withdrawal, could grow into a lasting sense of confusion and an irreversible alienation process.

427. Often, a partner might simply behave somewhat passively, while hoping to find a solution for their relationship. Then, the other partner reacts in a retaliatory manner out of spite. For example, he/she refuses to have sex until his/her partner responds to his/her needs. All along, they find each other's demands (and attitude) unrealistic or consider each other's seemingly retaliatory reactions a kind of blackmail. Thus, the game heats up. A partner's decent objective for a brief withdrawal—to signal his/her partner about a likely conflict between them—is misperceived and responded to harshly by the other.

428. During this process, the mental or sexual deprivation puts added pressures on partners. They take the threat to their needs for compassion and sex seriously and become hostile.

429. All along, the point ignored by both partners is that their partners might have had good intentions, at least initially. Both partners might have, in fact, been genuinely trying to salvage their relationship. Albeit they do not know how to make their points clear to each other.

430. All these conflicts and confusions are not necessarily even a matter of bad communication. Rather, couples are living in such an imaginary world they do not even grasp the nature of their problems, even though they insist that they do.

431. More importantly, they ignore that often it is merely their own personal needs and expectations that require adjusting, and not their partners' attitude.

432. As stated before, most of our personal needs are artificial in new societies, anyway. Our needs for more things and more compassion are what we have imposed upon ourselves by habit and imitation.

433. We have become too spoiled and demanding, because we believe we deserve better. We have become too ambitious and impatient. Our phony social values have made us too needy and desperate.

434. Thus, in most cases, merely our needs must be adjusted if we really wish to boost our relationships. We should simply learn to look at the bigger picture and stop fussing about our long list of artificial needs.

435. We must find ways of fulfilling our personal needs rather independently, so that the burdens on relationships subside.

436. People are normally better in retaliation than finding a means of reconciliation. This is human nature. This habit shows humans' inherent limitations.

437. We are unwilling to accept that our spouses often cannot fulfil our personal needs due to their unique characteristics and not necessarily out of spite.

438. Therefore, normally, partners' honourable intentions get lost amidst their psychological deprivations and clashes. Soon, partners face big catastrophes: Their personal needs are not

satisfied and they must face their partner's retaliations, too. Things get out of control. Relationships fall apart.

439. Often, we must either submit to our partner's demands, which are usually outside our means and beliefs, or prepare ourselves for further struggles and alienation. In either case, we introduce more destructive games and hostility into our relationships. Therefore, the war of nerves continues until our relationships are ruined. This is a typical and familiar scenario that ruins most relationships… But is it natural?

440. It can be counter-argued that relationship inconveniences are a fair price to pay for its advantages. Considering the benefits and the joy of relationships, we will continue to get ourselves into this tough conundrum repeatedly regardless of all the warnings.

441. Especially for younger people with all kinds of hopes and urges, relationships will continue to appear like a safe haven despite all the daunting evidences in society. They dismiss the high likelihood of future hardships for the sake of the immediate pleasure of someone's company *now*—another major repercussion of living in the now! Another sad fact!

442. All along, each partner in a relationship feels the burden of unfulfilled personal needs, plus the added demands of his/her partner to make him/her happy.

443. Moreover, a 'relationship' creates a variety of needs of its own, as will be explained in Chapter Eight. Most often these needs remain unrecognized and unfulfilled, which then stir added confusion for partners personally and in terms of relating to one another. The most obvious ones are created once children are brought into the equation.

444. Parents, already burdened by unfulfilled personal needs and their partners' demands, must suddenly face their children's needs, too. Moreover, they often have conflicting strategies for satisfying their children's needs as well.

445. On top of all this, children's needs are getting too complex and irrational these days anyhow. We are allowing, actually

encouraging, this spoiling norm without proper justification. This is all part of social pressure to give children more love and things every day, and because partners like to satisfy their own egos and their needs for the love of their children.

446. The children's needs also limit partners' time and ability to attend to their own personal needs. Thus, they get edgy and blame their partners for all these inconveniences, at least subconsciously. A symptom of partners' deprivation (for compassion) emerges when parents begin to compete and fight for the love of their children.

447. Each parent tries to prove his/her love to the children by spoiling them more, or even badmouthing and humiliating his/her partner. They do all these ridiculous crimes with the aim of satisfying their own personal need for compassion, which they hope to satisfy partially through their children at least.

448. Therefore, in every relationship, three sets of unfulfilled needs (personal needs, partners' demands, and relationship needs) place unmanageable pressures on both partners. Then, these subdued needs and demands keep piling up and causing more tension, clashes, and retaliations.

449. Nevertheless, we cannot avoid the temptation of getting into relationships, but we must become more conscious about its devastating pitfalls, too. We must be better equipped to deal with its inevitable hardships, and know how to get out of it —which most likely becomes necessary—with the least amount of damage.

450. Relationship environment's complexity and our passivity about it are the reasons why it will take at least a century, if at all, to find real solutions for relationships. Still, we can improve our relationships immediately by making moderate adjustments in our personal mentalities.

Chapter Seven
Facts about
Relationship Perceptions

All the facts noted so far reveal our misperceptions about life, our needs, and the purpose of relationships. Our outlooks are often erroneous and problematic, because we are naturally biased due to our genetics and cognition, while influenced by social conditioning, too. Accordingly, we often misjudge our partners and the health of our relationships, too. This chapter elaborates on the causes of our misperceptions and our role to recognize and remedy the obstacles they cause.

451. Our accurate views of corruption and duplicity in society raise our cynicism about people's sincerity and authenticity. Then, this personal wisdom (warranted defence mechanism) often leads to lots of misperceptions in relationships usually inadvertently, since every simple act by our spouses might appear suspicious and be misunderstood.
452. At the same time, many misperceptions are caused merely by our own idiosyncrasies and miscommunications.
453. Accordingly, conflicts arise in relationships quickly due to partners' misperceptions of themselves, their partners, their personal needs, and their relationship needs. Our warranted cynicism (mistrust) aggravates the matter as well.

454. Besides ruining our relationships, our miscommunications and misperceptions stir deep personal confusions about who we are, what we need, and what can make us happy.

455. At the same time, we cannot overcome our misperceptions readily due to our deep psychological constructs. Our firm inner forces, i.e., instincts, genetics, habits, and impulses, stir our dogmatic perceptions and decisions. This is a major factor (and obstacle) in relationships.

456. One major hurdle in relationships is that we cannot perceive even our own personalities accurately, yet judge each other hastily—mostly in line with our misperceptions and biases.

457. Meanwhile, we have become the most snobbish people on earth throughout the entire history of humanity due to our growing misperceptions of our capacities and needs.

458. We lose our identity when our perceptions of the world and our personality contradict reality largely. Meanwhile, a lack of personal identity raises confusion and misperceptions. It makes the job of adapting to our environment difficult and frustrating. This vicious cycle continues until we feel totally out of touch with reality, ourselves, and our living purposes.

459. Indeed, we never appreciate who we are despite our lifelong struggle to establish our identities. The simple reason is that we perceive ourselves and our personalities according to the inner forces shaping our attitudes, our biased perceptions of the world, and the bogus social values that we are striving to adopt or adapt to.

460. In relationships, the task of developing our identities faces even a tougher challenge. This happens because being in a relationship imposes a new puzzling role for partners just for the sake of making the best of the situation. And since partners like to influence (or humour) each other.

461. Besides its spiritual tone, 'Who am I?', as a philosophical question, reflects the complexity of our personalities and perceptions. We have all realized the difficulty of answering this question.

462. However, 'Who am I?' also reflects the existence of another *unknown* dimension of us, the self—our true being aside from our own or other people's perceptions of us.

463. We are responsible for misperceptions in relationships when we imagine knowing who we are, instead of making efforts to learn more about ourselves through self-awareness. We are also guilty for allowing our misperceptions cripple our grasp of our partners, means of communicating, and abilities to solve our conflicts.

464. As intelligent humans, we could assume that understanding our real needs and who we are is our main mission in life. However, we are not even used to self-analysis to realize the extent of our defects and faulty perceptions.

465. Not only we assume and insist that we know who we are, but also we insist that our partners are fully aware of who they are (mostly as we perceive them!).

466. Once we set our minds about 'who they are,' positively or negatively, it becomes almost impossible to accept any logic or counter argument about the validity of our opinions and perceptions.

467. If only we understand that our partners cannot learn what we insist they must learn, we may be able to better manage our relationships and assess our options realistically.

468. We are too self-centred in terms of not only thinking mostly about our needs, but also imposing them on our marriages.

469. Relationship conflicts reveal couples' rooted misperceptions about 'who they are and can be.' They just keep showing off a pompous identity to prove their strong individuality.

470. Our communications are driven by various impulses and/or motives at conscious, subconscious, and unconscious levels. Thus, the level of consciousness is a crucial psychological factor in our communications.

471. Mind and body are only tools to serve us. They are applied by this powerful entity called 'the Self' or 'Cognition' to run our affairs, partly consciously and partly unconsciously.

472. Cognition and consciousness are the locus of our attributes, behaviour, and decisions.

473. Our weaknesses and strengths are stored at many levels of consciousness. They affect us and people around us, either positively or negatively, depending on our awareness, which is simply the level of our consciousness and cognition that we have learned to master.

474. The importance of self-awareness becomes evident when we consider its objective to dig into our subconscious and unconscious territories and gradually explore the causes of our deep-rooted behaviour.

475. Self-awareness is also crucial for assessing our perceptions and refining our life outlook and mentality.

476. In particular, awareness helps us notice our insecurities and fears, e.g., about rejection and loneliness, or the overall risks of independent thinking and behaving. We learn we are too attached to society to dare resist its demands and values.

477. Humans' natural tendencies cause deep misperceptions for them, while social values and environment goad humans' inherent wickedness. No culture and ethical principles exists to guide people control their vile urges.

478. Most likely, the idea of human nature's purity is merely a fantasy—a huge misperception in itself. Humans, like other creatures in nature, are most likely supposed to be offensive and wild to protect themselves and their species. Except that humans are often careless about their own kind, too, as they keep killing one another in millions as a routine lifestyle—a justified habit. So far, we have only proven human nature's deep impurity.

479. Our search for tranquility and purity has just emerged from humans' struggle to escape constant suffering and stress.

480. In fact, we might have an easier task proving that humans become more arrogant and unreliable as time goes by. We should just defeat our misperceptions about our importance as a species!

481. These depressing conclusions about human nature further confirm the earlier points about human limitations to grasp the requirements of relationships and coping with them. *In fact, unfortunately, this author believes that human nature is not bad—it is horrible!*

482. Still, despite the hassles of social adaptation, some level of active involvement with life offers the opportunity of being a worthy human by learning to become a more conscious and conscientious person.

483. Most of our thoughts and decisions are processed beyond our control (in our subconscious and unconscious). The first benefit of this knowledge is that we appreciate the difficulty of effective communication more clearly. We recognize the obstacles of communicating and the destructive force of our misperceptions for running our relationships.

484. Learning about the levels of consciousness can enhance our objectivity, to judge our own and other people's behaviour better. More importantly, a few people might also acquire a capacity to tap the enormous power of subconscious and unconscious—towards enlightenment.

485. The three personality aspects of an individual match the three levels of consciousness very nicely. This reflects the correlation between a person's level of consciousness and his/her personality and behaviour in line with his/her daily perceptions and misperceptions.

486. The **Model** mostly operates from within the conscious level of one's mind. It represents mostly our sense of adaptation, playfulness, and sociability.

487. The **Ego** represents our subconscious mind, which holds our private and selfish traits and motives.

488. The **Self** represents mostly our unconscious urges, instincts, potentialities, and spirituality inclinations.

489. Miscommunications and misperceptions keep instigating one another and piling up fast in the early stages of relationships. Once these misperceptions are deposited in various levels of

couples' consciousness, they shape their Egos and Models, and thus very little people can do to control their crooked personalities or relationships.

490. Our communications, perceptions, and consciousness are vastly interrelated impulses in line with the three personality aspects. Collectively, they stir our reactions and behaviour in any circumstance.

491. Our misperceptions and Egos cripple us to distinguish the right success factors for maintaining our relationships.

492. Commonsense do not help us solve relationship conflicts, because everybody has his/her unique perception of logic. Nowadays, there seems to be as many varieties of logic and rules in relationships as people in them.

493. Couples are living in such an imaginary world (due to their misperceptions) they cannot even grasp the nature of their relationship problems, let alone finding solutions within that imaginary setting. Therefore, only some modern guidelines can help relationships prosper within some kind of orderly atmosphere.

494. Besides all the peculiar causes of misperceptions explained in this chapter, five main sources of misperceptions cause plenty of miscommunications and conflicts in relationships:

- Equivocation
- Misrepresentation
- Transference
- Apprehension
- Identity

These sources of relationship conundrums and the rather complex topic of perceptions are elaborated in this author's book, *The Nature of Love and Relationships*. Those rather technical discussions reveal the enormity of couples' rising misperceptions and their effects on their relationships.

Chapter Eight

Facts about

Relationship Needs

This chapter highlights some general facts about evolving relationship needs, models, and success factors, nowadays.[†]

495. As social values and couples' personal needs change during the course of history, the meaning, purpose, and format of their relationships should also be reassessed and redefined. The reason is that people's personal needs dictate the kind of relationships they are willing to accept for their novel lifestyles. Obviously, the changes in lifestyle and personal needs in the last few decades have been enormous. Yet, we have not developed a reasonably compatible framework for our relationships, hence the hectic situation we are facing. The fast-changing nature of relationships in the new era and emerging trends are outlined in Part II and our relationship choices are discussed in Part III.

496. We should learn to view 'relationships' as a unique entity, which has specific needs very different from the conflicting needs of two partners.

497. We can say that *a relationship is a collection of partners' actions and feelings*. However, a relationship should also be

---

[†] Details regarding these topics are available in this author's book, *Relationships Needs, Framework, and Models*.

viewed as a *system or atmosphere for facilitating partners' cooperation to achieve certain goals.*

498. Presently, no uniform set of objectives is available to guide couples in their relationships and tame their wild perceptions of relationships' potentials and purposes.

499. Without a practical framework, the state of relationships would deteriorate beyond control very soon.

500. Without guidelines, even compatible couples are subject to gross misperceptions and loose views of their relationships. (Relationship guidelines are explained in Chapter Thirteen.)

501. A big goal of building a framework is to discuss and purge the gross misperceptions in society about relationships.

502. The framework can help partners learn some guidelines to 'relate' to each other, instead of hoping to *relate* naturally or through a lifelong trials and errors. The framework would assist couples establish their objectives and expectations from relationships more realistically.

503. Another objective of the relationship framework is to offer a handful relationship models that can fit individuals' varied personalities, while fulfilling some general advantages of being in relationships.

504. Realistically, couples must evaluate their personal needs in comparison with relationships' unique needs objectively, and then choose a proper relationship model that best fits their personalities.

505. Of course, every relationship has its unique characteristics and setting. And there should be some level of flexibility in relationship guidelines to accommodate all personalities. Yet, only a handful relationship models can support partners to relate to each other effectively.

506. Couples' stress due to new lifestyles and misperceptions are crippling a good majority of relationships, while threatening the foundation of our societies in general, too. The situation will only worsen if revolutionary solutions and a framework for relationships are not found soon.

507. The first step for developing a framework is to accept and redefine relationships as an *independent* setting, and not a collection of partners' erratic whims.

508. People are paranoid about fairness, nowadays. A progressive 'relationship framework' can replace the need for couples' constant fight for 'equality.'

509. The main objectives of a relationship framework are to:

- Enforce teamwork.
- Bring objectivity back into relationships.
- Increase communication effectiveness.
- Reduce partners' expectations from relationships.
- Overhaul couples' mentalities and social mechanisms.

510. Knowing about teamwork and actually being committed to it, as the only solution for relationships, are different things.

511. For the mere reason that individuality is becoming the most crucial requirement of relationships, building new methods of teamwork is imperative more than ever.

512. New methods of teamwork might include a variety of tools, including a simple agreement between partners for sharing marital and financial responsibilities and sticking to the plan.

513. Another role of teamwork is to maintain a balance between partners' personal needs in line with the relationship needs.

514. Once partners learn to focus on teamwork, their obsession for *equality* becomes obsolete. Instead of relying on equality, or superiority, the success of relationships would be gauged only by the smooth operation and outcome of teamwork.

515. Indeed, the strength of teamwork lies on its emphasis on partners' independence and objectivity.

516. In line with our personal obsessions for more affection and things, we have reduced the capacity of our relationships to be objective.

517. Without guidelines and principles, couples' communications have become subjective, egotistical, emotional, and futile.

518. The logic says that the more we promote individuality, the less everybody should expect from, or rely on, relationships. Instead, we must become more self-reliant and independent.

519. A major task for partners is to remember that their personal needs and relationship needs are not the same or parallel.

520. They must remember that most relationship problems and misperceptions erupt because couples perceive relationship needs as an extension of their personal needs.

521. Thus, lots of soul searching and mental growth are needed in order to adapt our relationships to new social framework.

522. We need modern thinking and principles for relationships to match the modern life we are so eagerly embracing.

523. Especially, the prevalent publicity around positive thinking has had disturbing effects on our views of life. We have lost touch with the harsh reality of life and believe we deserve all the best of everything, including a flawless relationship. We have all become too spoiled and idealistic.

524. We look for an imaginary idol to accept as our companion or we try to rebuild (change) our partners to fit that image. Especially, a trend is out there to make men softer, so they can fit women's desires and perceptions of relationships.

525. Everybody is unique (and most likely damaged) due to his/her flawed nature, needs, and perceptions. Thus, people's expectation to find or create their ideal partners is just naïve. It is amazing how partners expect each other to act, think and feel like them, as if such transformation was feasible or even desirable.

526. The question partners must ask themselves is whether they can find the right formula—relationship model—to relate to each other effectively and live a quiet life without trying to change each other.

527. We seldom get a chance to learn about the finer means of thinking and living. Even when we do, we have a hard time staying on a path of awareness when people around us are consumed with superficial needs and spread phony values.

528. Instead of seeking an ideal relationship setting, maybe our new goal should be to make relationships only manageable and tolerable. This requires conscious efforts to lower our expectations and find viable objectives for our relationships.
529. At two extremes, a relationship may be viewed as a spiritual connection between two individuals, or a boring obligation between them to share life's hardships.
530. We might perceive relationships as a sacred experience in beauty and selflessness, or only a means of social adaptation and self-gratification. While the latter feels closer to reality, the former reflects our innate, spiritual search for perfection.
531. In new societies, people's perceptions of relationships cover both of the above two extremes and lots more between them. In particular, more people, nowadays, strive to find their soul mates, while at the same time they are unable to cope even with their relationships' basic needs.
532. Accordingly, we have no clear picture of what relationships are supposed to be (or can be). We merely try to bring some degree of both practicality and romance to our relationships.
533. Yet, we seem incapable to find the right balance between practicality and romance. For instance, most people realize that a prenuptial agreement is useful as a practical measure, but doing so still feels businesslike and unromantic to them.
534. We often fail to use logic when it is wise to be practical, and we do not know how to express our emotions when it can sweeten a relationship. Thus, we have been unable to bring either practicality or romance into our crude relationships. The reason is that social changes have been too drastic and misleading in the new era, while tainting our personalities, perceptions of the world, and relationships.
535. We have become too spoiled, needy, and impatient, while our relentless search for a reliable companion is raising our confusion, mistrust, and depression.
536. The truth is that our *urgent* emotional *needs* (e.g., needs for sex, ELove, and security) overpower our abilities to think

practically about the potential catastrophes of relationships. This is particularly true since our spirits is usually weakened by other harsh realities of modern lifestyles already.

537. Tension is growing in relationships due to not only people's higher emphasis on independence, but also their ongoing self-pity for not having an ideal partner in their lives.

538. Nowadays, people have a high opinion of themselves (often unrealistically), thus set a high standard for an ideal partner and their needs from relationships.

539. People like to exaggerate their self-worth to themselves and others in order to prove their *presumed* identity.

540. People's showy zeal for individualism (identity), nowadays, raises their inner conflicts, since the more they play phony roles for being popular or assertive with a fake personality, the more they lose their innate identity

541. Every day, life is getting harder to tolerate, especially due to relationships' vile atmosphere raising our inabilities to adapt socially and emotionally in a natural way.

542. People seem obsessed with their search for a soul mate, nowadays, as they consider it a necessity and a right.

543. However, having a companion feels like a lot of work these days, too, and often the cause of more stress.

544. The level and complexity of partners' expectations have kept increasing as society promotes phonier lifestyles.

545. Realistically, however, people's level of expectations from relationships should be reduced to compensate for the rising social pressures on people's personal lives already.

546. As normal human beings, we are unable to respond to our rotating needs for independence and dependence.

547. Even worse, we are usually unable to respond to the rotating demands of our partners for independence and dependence.

548. Therefore, we must adopt a relationship model to mitigate the effects of our inability to cope with all these imbalances between partners' somewhat random, but persistent, needs for both independence and dependence.

549. The existing social fervour for independence indicates that, as a rule, couples should emphasize on a relationship model that best guarantees partners' independence.

550. The higher we climb up the 'relationship needs tree,' a higher sense of dependence and maturity is required from partners. Accordingly, couples' high urge for independence means that they should stick to models in the lower levels of the relationship needs tree.

551. The 'relationship needs tree' and five simple relationship models are presented in more detail in *the Nature of Love and Relationships*. Yet, those models can be expanded and explained in a working manual. Couples can then use that manual to identify the model most suitable for them. Instead of the five models suggested in that book, possibly a tree with about a dozen relationship models can be designed.

552. Advocating independence in relationships might appear in contrast with the aim of 'enforcing teamwork.' However, there is no conflict here, as 'teamwork' must be viewed as an objective negotiation process between two independent partners and not their dependency urges.

553. Often our 'psychological construct' dictates the urgency of our needs. Therefore, the 'need urgency' concept suggests that, for many of us, being at a certain level of 'personal needs tree' is so urgent and important we can ignore all other needs, even if we face starvation or death.

554. All personal needs demand our attention at some degree and time. Yet, our need for a companion seems to be an urgent, everlasting, and imposing need, more like a basic need.

555. When couples cannot create a good balance between their personal needs and the relationship needs, they feel tension. Thus, each partner must convince him/herself honestly about his/her real needs, instead of merely accommodating his/her partner by accepting a general relationship model hastily.

556. Partners may leave some room for leniency in terms of the relationship model they are comfortable with, but not too

much at the cost of going against their natural needs, e.g., need for independence. When partners cannot agree on a reasonable compromise about a suitable relationship model for them, the situation offers the best indication that they are not made to be in a relationship together.

557. Although couples must have the option of choosing the best relationship model for their personalities and needs, they should start from the simplest relationship model that is the lowest in the relationship tree, i.e., highest independence for partners with the minimum level of expectations. They can then try to climb up the tree gradually according to their real experiences in their relationships and by demonstrating their aptitude and personality strengths.

558. The relationship framework and mechanisms proposed in this book (Part III) put the onus on partners to be vigilant about their relationships and choose the right relationship model for them at the outset. It is their own fault if they get themselves involved in faulty relationships or do not end them quickly and peacefully.

559. In this setting, partners have a proactive and progressive mindset. Most importantly, partners view their relationship as a temporary arrangement, unless they can prove their true expertise and sincerity to work together.

560. Relationships can no longer be viewed as a whimsical set of couples' activities and needs to merely fulfil their emotional deficiencies. Being in a relationship is a serious *business* and must be viewed as such by partners.

561. The factors for success in relationships are quite different, nowadays, and they would most likely keep changing in the future according to changes in social structure. Therefore, our approach to relationships' format, needs, models, and success should reflect this reality.

PART II

Relationship Trends

Chapter Nine
Fundamental Trends

So many unhinging changes and trends in society have affected relationships deeply. These revelations have mostly transpired in people's rising personal needs and expectations from life and marriage. Now, societies have become satiated with progressive philosophies and mottos that have induced grave misperceptions about life's purposes and relationships' potentials. Thus, for assessing the prospect of relationships, we must gauge social trends and their impacts, and then develop relationship principles in line with people's modern attitudes. Part II discusses these trends. Then, some radical solutions are offered in Part III to address our rampant personal needs and review our choices for coping within modern relationships.

562. A fundamental, emerging trend, nowadays, is that we value our freedom and identity a lot. We give the highest level of emphasis to our personal need for independence more than ever in human history. Now, this new mentality affects our relationships the most.

563. Many reasons exist for this *supposedly civilized* mentality, but the women's equal rights stands out the most. Due to their efforts, now everybody is keener about his/her need for independence and identity. Therefore, this major premise,

i.e., the need for independence, should be our best guide in developing new relationship principles.

564. At the same time, we have the least amount of expertise and stamina to actually live independently, mostly due to our extreme need for dependence as well (as discussed in Chapter Four), and all the induced inner conflicts.

565. The second fundamental development is that, nowadays, people are constantly playing various roles and games to portray an appealing personality, mask their idiosyncrasies, adapt to social values and demands, and manipulate (and control) others.

566. The contradiction between the above two prominent trends, i.e., people's drive for independence (identity) and their tendency to play phony roles to be popular, creates another big set of inner conflicts for them. This is because the more they try to prove their identities through superficial means, the phonier they become and the more they lose a chance to find their Self or a reliable companion.

567. Thus, a majority of people are losing their touch with both life and their identities more every day due to not only their overall misperceptions, but also the roles and games they are forced to play to be popular and accepted in society.

568. For one thing, we exaggerate our self-worth to others and ourselves to prove our wisdom and importance. Thus, we are not authentic and sincere enough even for building our identities, let alone a reliable social image. We have indeed become quite estranged with our true nature.

569. This debilitating condition has created all kinds of problems for us for finding the right companion, communicating, and maintaining our marriages. Meanwhile, we appear even less capable to define our identities without reliable partners.

570. The situation gets worse when counsellors make couples play still another category of roles to solve their relationship conflicts. These new roles create even more confusion for people about who they are and how they should be relating

to their partners. People's habitual, unauthentic roles and games are at least familiar to them and partially justified emotionally and intellectually. However, their new roles (suggested by counsellors) often cause them more anxiety, as they contradict both partners' existing roles and true nature.

571. The third fundamental new trend in society is that couples place a much higher emphasis on their personal needs than relationship needs. In fact, they are hardly even aware that certain relationship needs exist, which must be satisfied way ahead of partners' needs.

572. Thus, couples naively expect reliable relationships (maybe even ideal ones based on their dreams) that can also help them achieve their weird goals and needs. If a relationship cannot fulfil these high expectations, they want out.

573. We are no longer willing to tolerate mediocre relationships. We are now more important than our relationships. Some readers may wonder if this has not been the case before. No, our old values inherently placed the needs of relationships ahead of individuals in line with traditions and religions. However, we are now past those outmoded systems.

574. Now individuals wish to be much more important than their relationships. We keep insisting that life is too short and we live only once. Therefore, we wish to take advantage of life as much as possible before it is too late. Thus, we sacrifice our relationships in the process quite readily.

575. In a nutshell, in the older times, the emphasis was put on 'survival,' whereas the emphasis is placed on 'happiness,' nowadays. (By the way, 'survival' is still the main goal of relationships in less modernized countries where people are facing pressing life dilemmas.)

576. Of course, our emphasis on happiness does not mean that we are happier people than past generations or those living in less spoiled countries. Rather, we just like to think (and pretend) we are happier. We want to show our resolve to find that elusive happiness. Why?

577. There are three major reasons for our incessant quest for happiness: **First,** we have been brainwashed to believe that happiness is out there and we can easily find it by satisfying our artificial needs for wealth, power, and love. Therefore, we keep struggling to satisfy these artificial needs with no end in sight or real happiness in our hearts. In fact, we are becoming more depressed every day, as we introduce more artificial needs in our lives, lose touch with reality, exhaust ourselves for vanity, and still fail to feel that illusive, dicey happiness, anyway. **Second,** we have been learning and propagating a lot of philosophy about life and happiness in recent decades. We like to talk a lot about happiness and prove our ability and conviction to build a happy life. All these exaggerated ideas about positive thinking, living in the now, and similar philosophies are ruining our abilities to perceive reality. **Third,** the rising depression and suffering in society make us more edgy and eager to find happiness, thus we become more susceptible to these naive mottos, too.

578. As societies grow, we suffer more, thus look for salvation (happiness) more obsessively. Actually, the above noted three reasons are interrelated. They have evolved to support (and incite) one another: That is, we strive to avoid (deny) reality by making up all kinds of philosophies in order to mitigate our suffering.

579. The above trends reflect our new mentality. And we cannot change it. Thus, our challenge is to develop relationship principles that fit this new reality (perceptions).

580. Another fundamental trend is that the old premise to depend on partners' romantic vows to love and cherish each other forever regardless of health and wealth is no longer helping them. Our daily experiences confirm that it is not working anymore. So, let us be honest about these facts. Those good (or bad) old days are long gone.

581. Another major trend is that, in recent decades, old values and relationship guidelines have been eradicated without

new ones replacing them. Even that limited old wisdom is now abolished. Instead, we have merely developed more unrealistic expectations for our relationships every year.

582. Moreover, we make subjective judgments about the health of our relationships merely based on personal perceptions and needs.

583. To avoid these misleading approaches and reverse some of the troubling trends, we need a simple set of relationship guidelines that makes enough sense to everybody and fits our new social realities.

The above rampant trends and lifestyle changes have tainted people's mentalities about their personal needs, which then affect their behaviour in their relationships. Accordingly, many other related trends are also noticeable in the new era:

584. People's expectations from relationships have skyrocketed erratically, because, i) they view relationship needs merely an extension of their personal needs, and, ii) they envisage relationships mostly a means of finding happiness.

585. Accordingly, the irrational rise of social intricacies, phony personal needs, egotism, and sexuality have made marriages too convoluted to define or bear.

586. Meanwhile, people's stress level keeps rising every year in line with their unfulfilled expectations and growing marital conflicts, while socioeconomic and career demands also put many pressures on couples.

587. Nowadays, people find their relationships less bearable than what they had imagined them at the outset.

588. People's inner conflicts and agony also keep increasing due to their growing sense of loneliness and insecurity, whether they have a partner or not.

589. All along, people's needs (obsession) for both independence and dependence will continue to rise as well. Accordingly, couples find less ground to relate and work as a team.

590. Each partner deems his/her individuality and independence the most crucial needs, in and outside of their relationship. They consider themselves too important and deserving to live a full and happy life. Thus, if relationships hinder these needs in some ways, they always choose their welfare above that of their partner and relationship as a whole. They want out if their relationships hinder their aspirations even slightly. Even worse, they abandon their relationships only based on some idiotic personal beliefs or obsessions.

591. Therefore, the rate of relationship failures will continue to climb, as people's personal needs as well as their urges for competition, independence, and superiority grow too fast in line with the increase in social complexity.

592. Considering the above trends, couples' commitment to their partners and relationships is at best conditional. They stay in their relationships only as long as their partners can satisfy their naive personal needs and keep them happy in line with their misperceived expectations from relationships.

593. People also gauge their relationships' strength based on their selfish perceptions and shallow values, since no principles exist, nowadays, to guide relationships or asses their health.

594. People's current approach and attitude fuels the process of social deterioration, while couples face evermore conflicts in relationships and become more impatient, too.

595. The above rampant trends are tangled in a vicious cycle and we must expect more social chaos and sufferings all along.

In line with the above fundamental trends, the basic nature of relationships is changing faster than ever as well, thus another set of clear trends are emerging, as listed below:

596. Nowadays, most people do not look for a partner to satisfy merely their basic companionship need. Rather, they want their relationships make them happy, satisfy a host of their personal needs, and solve their personal problems; all based

on their juvenile misperceptions regarding the purpose and capacity of relationships. Meanwhile, they also blame their relationships for their personal failure to find happiness and peace.

597. Couples are behaving more like rivals, trying to outdo and manipulate each other, instead of acting like caring partners capable of stirring teamwork and synergy to make the best of their relationships.

598. Personal idiosyncrasies and insecurities have kept rising as social values have deteriorated, and vice versa. This vicious cycle would continue to spin out of control and make the success of relationships less likely every year.

599. Couples' insecurity and need for retaliation have reached such extremes that they kidnap, terrorize, or harm their own children just for intimidating their estranged spouses. The intensity of child custody and separation battles also shows how ineffective our relationship mechanisms are.

600. The possibility of finding our soul mates is getting slimmer every year. Yet, we keep struggling and stressing ourselves more, because of our sense of loneliness and desire to stay positive. Our romantic search for a soul mate is preventing us from perceiving relationships realistically.

601. For keeping a reliable companion (let alone a soul mate), partners should have many common interests, be good and compatible humans, make lots of compromises, and work on their relationships' needs constantly. However, human nature does not support these requirements. In fact, the trend shows that we are getting more arrogant and greedy every year, thus making ourselves less capable of getting along.

602. Considering the above trends and hundreds of other reasons explained in this book, marriage would continue to become less stable and manageable every year. Thus, it seems more necessary to view marriages as a temporary arrangement, unless both partners gain all the high qualities required for building an effective relationship.

Chapter Ten
Moral and Social Trends

All the facts and trends noted in the previous nine chapters reveal the intensity of social decline and its adverse effects on humans' morality, morale, and happiness. However, we have neither taken the time to grasp the nature of new relationships, nor seem eager to develop sensible guidelines and mechanisms for relationships in line with the requirements of new lifestyles. Accordingly, we can see the following social and moral trends:

603. We have now created a heinous society guided by all kinds of shallow ideals and slogans to manage our hectic lives and relationships, especially our marriages. This is getting really too embarrassing for the presumably intelligent humans.
604. Even after we grasp the roots of marital problems and social mayhem, we do not adjust our mentalities or envision the need for workable social and relationship mechanisms.
605. Instead, we try to handle the symptoms of marital conflicts and breakdowns thru marriage counselling, by playing phony roles and games, or by resorting to shoddy rules and laws.
606. Thus, it seems it would take us centuries to grasp the depth of relationship conundrums, if at all. It would take us even longer to prepare and propagate a new framework that can help couples relate more effectively.
607. Proposing any timeframe for reversing the deteriorating trends in relationships would be subjective. Yet, if someone insisted to know the author's most optimistic predictions, he would offer the following estimates and dates:

A) By the year 2115, couples and society will develop a reasonable grasp of relationship hurdles and implement the needed radical changes.

B) By 2150, tangible progress in relationships will be witnessed globally, providing more catastrophic events, such as climate and economy, do not distract us altogether.

608. Suggesting the above, or any, dates sounds ridiculous, even to the author himself, considering the dismal prospects of humanity in general if we follow our present path. Social challenges facing us in terms of water and food shortage, global warming effects, the rising sea levels, looming wars, and numerous other natural and manmade catastrophes may bring humanity to its knees in only a few decades, anyway.

609. Our distraction by various socioeconomic issues is indeed another reason that relationship problems might not be dealt with in any speeder manner, if at all.

610. On the other hand, the scope of social catastrophes might automatically reduce our expectations from relationships a lot when we are forced to focus on the matter of survival, somewhat like the humans of the Stone Age. In that setting, the present fuss over personal needs and happiness would be thrown out the window.

611. Nonetheless, we must plan according to our most optimistic assumptions about the future of humanity. We should keep some faith in humans' resilience and eventual awakening to face the variety of problems we have created for ourselves and our relationships.

612. The criteria to gauge improvements in relationships consist of lower divorce rates, less hostility and stress in families, a better balance between personal needs and the relationship needs, and better societies.

Is Year 2115 a Good Target?

Considering the fast deteriorating situation of relationships and the rising personal stress due to socioeconomic conditions, the year 2115 seems like a reasonable ballpark to see an active change of attitude towards relationships. On the other hand, we can improve our relationships personally right away if we adopt a rather progressive mentality and behave more realistically in line with the facts suggested in this book.

Some readers may find 2115 too pessimistic. They could argue that if real problems existed in relationships, people would tackle them quickly rather than wait over a century to help themselves. Actually, they might suggest the situation would auto-correct itself if a real need for change becomes evident. However, various discussions in this book show why our personal interests and flawed reasoning stand in our way of giving a higher priority to sanitizing our relationships. In particular, it seems plausible to anticipate the following trends:

613. Humans' innate arrogance and dogmatism always demolish our senses to act realistically and logically, especially when we try to relate to one another. Our modern preoccupation with individualism, equality, and self-gratification reflects the new trend about humans' dire obsession for controversy.
614. Marital environment is not going to auto-correct itself, as many conflicting forces besiege relationships these days and prevent any rational development of practical ideas. Rather, a scientific intervention should stir everybody's awareness and willingness to learn about and improve relationships.
615. On the other hand, it would probably take us a long time to eventually realize the need for a set of Generally Acceptable Relationship Principles (GARP) and related mechanisms.
616. Even then, it will take a long time before GARP and other relationship ideas are adopted and functional. The reasons are obvious: People are, nowadays, too preoccupied with

many complex, daily routines to take GARP seriously. We are not experts in finding solutions, and we have too rigid mindsets to accept radical changes. Ironically, only few of us seem worried enough regarding the depth of relationship problems, anyway, in spite of the overwhelming evidences before our eyes and the sufferings we endure.

617. It appears that we have a great appetite for denial in order to sustain our hopes for finding love and happiness eventually. Our sad experiences with our love affairs are not teaching us much about the repercussions of our romanticism.

618. On top of our chronic naiveté, social mechanisms are not progressive enough in line with social changes and couples' demand for independence and individuality. In particular, social mechanisms, mostly legal systems, should be adapted to the new social realities, so that people can adjust their mindsets, too.

619. Some magical forces might cause faster improvement in the state of relationships and societies. Some people or scholars might even believe that the existing situation would become tolerable with few minor modifications that couples can learn to make in their relationships quickly. Yet, the author doubts these possibilities. Again, the chance for some kind of auto-correction looks low to the author. On the contrary, the need for direct intervention of scholars and governments seems inevitable if we wish to become more civilized and suffer less in our relationships.

620. On the other hand, some people and scholars may find the suggested above dates of 2115 and 2150 too optimistic. They probably have many good arguments to support their claims. The author is rather inclined to agree with them. However, let us take a middle ground and hope that some kinds of solutions can be envisioned by the next century. Nonetheless, choosing a date is not meant to be scientific or essential, but rather a scheme to reflect the difficulty of the job at hand as far as the author can say.

621. In order to be a little bit more specific about the question 'Why 2115,' however, we must study the following topics:

- The ***socioeconomic trends*** regarding relationships (noted in this chapter),
- The ***emerging relationship circumstances*** in the new era (presented in the next chapter), and
- A reasonable (tentative) timetable for ***implementing radical remedies*** to bring some order to relationships (presented in Chapter Fourteen).

The following **Socioeconomic Trends** are evident, nowadays:

622. Our economic systems, mainly consumerism, are deforming social values. People have gained a big appetite for objects, ideologies, and wealth, all in hopes of capturing that elusive happiness, even at the cost of damaging their marriages.

623. 'Life is too short' and 'You live only once' have become the main mottos for most of us. Therefore, people jump out of their relationships to find a better partner and enjoy their presumed short lives the best they can. Meanwhile, the main requirements of relationships are ignored in the clouds of confusing slogans, misperceptions, and superficial values.

624. The increase in personal needs (for objects and compassion) has directly resulted in the decline of both moral and morale in society, while couples have raised their expectations from relationships enormously, too.

625. The impact of higher expectations from relationships has been two folds: First, it has stirred added personal stress that infects relationships. Second, we have come to believe that relationships can fulfil many of our emotional and financial needs. Couples assume their partners are psychologically capable of providing all the love they seek. They demand more attention and affection to soothe their personal hurts and the stress of living in a chaotic world. Thus, in effect, they are weakening the potency of their relationships.

626. Couples try to live beyond their means, at a higher standard of living than they can afford or deserve. This is an added source of pressure, while partners strive to find that elusive happiness at all cost. They demand more regardless of their means. Family debt per capita in relation to their income is at its highest level ever, due to crooked family values and consumerism. Family crises are getting out of hand due to the lack of partners' sensibility about budgeting and money.

627. New societies have advocated the concepts of equality and individualism. Partners' drive for independence and identity has turned relationships into a battleground for couples to set their territories and superiorities. Thus, the role of teamwork in relationships is not gaining the needed steam and care.

628. Couples abandon their relationships readily by the simplest signs of inconvenience. They want to give themselves the highest chance of finding happiness in another relationship as soon as possible.

629. No longer are any principles available to guide couples, nor any standards exist to measure the health of relationships. Therefore, couples rely on their own subjective viewpoints or the advice of friends and family to justify their crooked conclusions about the state of their relationships.

630. Couples consider 'love' the main factor for relationships' success, not only for starting one, but also for sustaining it. The problem with this approach has been discussed in detail in Chapter Four and other parts of this book.

631. Relationships have become too complex to grasp and too demanding to cope with. Meanwhile, couples are not even trained about the basic relationship needs, the psychological effects of their encounters, and how deeply they are affected by their genes and rearing conditions. They do not realize that people's mindsets or personalities cannot be changed simply because their partners are expecting them to change.

632. The level of angst and stress in the surviving relationships is growing, too, due to partners' oversensitivity and unfulfilled

expectations from relationships. Partners are also burdened by their warranted indecision about staying in, or leaving, their dysfunctional relationships.

633. The number of divorces and separations has skyrocketed in the last few decades in line with the emerging social trends without raising adequate alarm or awareness in society.

634. Stress levels in society and organizations have increased drastically due to the complexity of work and interactions, employment uncertainties, discriminations, international competition, and managers' obsession to serve themselves, instead of attending to their social responsibilities.

635. Accordingly, the stress level in families has also increased, because, nowadays, usually both spouses work outside the house and are exposed to extreme pressures, especially women, who have been subject to more discrimination and abuse in organizations.

636. Bad values and habits of organizations, such as hypocrisy, power struggle, and arrogance have infected relationships, too. Partners follow the same rules to assert themselves at work and at home. Some women might actually perceive their husbands as abusive bosses in the work environment as well as at home.

637. Personal stress because of social demands and substandard relationships makes couples testy and impatient. They bug each other exactly at the time that life is confusing enough and out of control already. Yet, they still expect each other to be more romantic, sincere, and trustworthy as well!

638. To remedy relationship problems and stir communication, counsellors encourage role-playing and love expressions. Yet, relationship problems keep rising. This trend shows that the existing schemes, especially role-playing, are not working. Logically, relationship conflicts would only rise, unless partners are naturally convinced about the feelings or words they exchange. In fact, all these role-playings, as well

as phony values, have made couples lose their identities and authenticities even faster in recent decades.

639. Companionship is probably the most important (basic) need of individuals, nowadays, and the one that is most often left unfulfilled. The importance of 'need for a companion' is evident in the wide range of personal needs it could satisfy potentially, as discussed in Chapter Four. Most people think and dream about a good companion as much as they think about food, consciously or subconsciously.

640. A crucial trend that couples ignore, when they look for or choose a partner, is that finding a soul mate usually turns into a sour fate since couples usually end up in substandard relationships. They have no inkling about the fact that **these days the chances of relationships failing are higher than surviving.** Couples ignore this vital reality at the outset and do not do enough soul-searching and planning.

641. Couples are untrained and unprepared to handle either the relationship needs, or relationships' most likely scenario, i.e., separation.

Chapter Eleven
Behavioural and Gender Trends

The socioeconomic trends noted in the last chapter mixed with humans' genetical and acquired wickedness discussed so far in this book reflect the sad prospect of relationships in the new era and the way everybody must endure more sufferings and stress due to social vanity. This chapter provides another 160 emerging trends regarding the vast changes in peoples' personalities, which have then led to wider gender differences and conflicts. These particularly disturbing trends reflect the emergence of complex dilemmas in relationship environment. They also reveal that reversing the deteriorating situation of relationships would be a long, uphill struggle. The way we think and act in society and relationships are getting bizarre. In particular, men and women's mindset and behaviour related to their love and relationship needs have shaped in odd ways in the new era in line with drastic changes in social values and new culture. Accordingly, gender differences and attitudes are also getting more complex and contentious with likely terrible upshots, thus this topic demands some scrutiny in this chapter. **The references to 'people', 'men', 'women', or 'we' in the book—mostly this chapter—do not mean that whole group, but rather a big portion of that category or gender.**

Behavioural Implications

642. People seem to be living in a fantasy world with substantial needs and dreams. Their ambitions and needs for objects do not necessarily match their talents and efforts, and their needs for affection do not match their capacity to exchange compassion. Even when they have wealth and compassion, they abuse them because they are not mentally prepared to handle them responsibly. The more their selfish needs are satisfied, the more arrogant and greedier they become. Yet, everybody believes he/she deserves more love and things.

643. Accordingly, the rising amount of unfulfilled expectations from relationships has led to lots of frustration, retaliation, and hostility in families and society. Furthermore, partners' oversensitivity due to untamed expectations has obscured even simple communications. For example, we hear often, nowadays, especially from women, a phrase such as, "He/she does not know how to spoil me!" Many flourishing relationships break down every day because of this bizarre expectation. They do not even mind saying it so bluntly, as though 'spoiling' is a reasonable demand for relationships now. Especially, after years of exploitation by men, now women want to be spoiled, as though making up (or taking revenge) for past generations' deprivations. They demand attention, ELove, and often obedience, seriously, or maybe even arrogantly on some occasions.

644. Meanwhile, couples' rising sexuality, superficial needs, and naive expectations from relationships have tainted people's characters and integrities as well as gender's ability to relate. Accordingly, these fast changes have placed extra pressures on the social structure and lowered its capacity to provide public services and maintain a healthy environment.

645. The amount of misperceptions and miscommunications in relationships are also increasing very fast and creating more havoc, as explained in Chapter Seven.

646. Most crucially, couples have lost their objectivity about the purposes and potentials of relationships, because they have become too idealistic and emotional about their expectations from relationships.

647. As a result, couples keep jumping out of their relationships faster and faster because they dream they can find another partner to fulfil their expectations better and give them the love and attention they believe they totally deserve.

648. Thus, most of us struggle all our lives in search of an ideal relationship. Only a few of us might eventually realize our naivety after repeated failures.

649. Both single and married people envy each other's position and lifestyle. We all desire the merits of both lifestyles now.

650. Married people do not appreciate the basic merits of their relationships because of their misperceptions about a single (independent) life and the possibility of finding love and happiness with a more suitable mate.

651. And unmarried people look for ideal partners obsessively to fill the gap in their lives, while they like to brag about their freedom as single persons.

652. Besides our pleasure seeking mentalities in the new era, our erratic urges for both dependence and independence play a big role in creating vast misperceptions about relationships.

653. A disturbing feature of relationships in the new era relates to partners' growing appetite for playing games in order to manipulate each other. The nature and extent of these games are becoming too complex and exhausting, thus making partners even more jittery and incompatible for building a sensible teamwork-oriented relationship together.

654. A main motive for these games is partners' potent needs for self-expression and retaliation, which are newly developed defence mechanisms that couples have adopted in order to supposedly protect themselves.

655. Couples play these games and roles to maintain the balance of power in their relationships. This is an ongoing, onerous

process, because partners simply seem incapable of putting down their guards, to live and relate naturally.

656. Almost everybody plays games and roles in society all his/her life to: 1) impress (charm), 2) flatter, 3) intimidate, or 4) snub someone. Therefore, the amount of time we are natural and sincere is minimal.

657. Hence, we are also forced to play games and roles all our lives. We are somehow dragged into situations beyond our control where we must play along with others and assert ourselves. Hardly anybody is natural these days. Even worse, some of us might also suffer deeply for being forced into this self-degrading, frustrating superficiality. This condition is also infecting relationships, as partners feel obliged to play games and roles constantly—out of necessity, sadly.

658. Another dilemma is that even when a partner decides to stop playing games and behave naturally, he/she still cannot handle his/her partner who is addicted to these relationship games.

659. The irony is that we all notice and criticize other people's games and phoniness fast, but ignore our own. Most often, we are subconsciously aware of the games and roles we are playing, but naively assume we can get away with them. We believe in our playacting too much. Or even worse, we think people are too simple or busy to see through our acts.

660. People also play roles and games in order to maximize their relationships' chances for success. However, by doing so, they actually increase the chances of being discredited and rejected.

661. A frustrating situation in relationships develops when a partner insists on playing a role or game and his/her partner is not falling for it.

662. Relationships fail since too many of partners' games keep clashing. The more games they play to cope with social and relationship issues, the more conflicts arise, which then lead to even more games and clashes.

663. Usually one partner starts a game with a special intention. Then the other partner starts his/her own game, instead of playing along. The first partner is astonished that his/her game is detected and resisted. They keep introducing more games until they are exhausted and angry.

664. People consider charming and manipulating others as their rights and an effective tool, while they believe they are good at it, too. So when they fail, they get upset and nasty about it. All that charm swiftly turns into hostility and ruins even their basic friendships or means of relating.

665. The way people snub each other like a pervasive game in hopes of relating—mostly for setting the tone of their social or marital relationships and boost their egos—is funny.

666. While the need for control is inherent in humans, it becomes even more prevalent and damaging in close relationships.

667. We try to control our partners to minimize the possibility of getting hurt by them, but also because we believe this would be the best way to protect our relationships.

668. Because of all these games and phony roles, nowadays, too many people are often struggling to either find a companion or get rid of him/her.

669. Thus, instead of expecting happiness from relationships, couples should actually be willing to pay a big price for it. This is a significant fact they must accept before entering a relationship. Always a high price must be paid for the few fringe benefits of relationships.

670. We must be prepared to absorb the normal disappointments in relationships without resorting to retaliation and useless quarrels.

671. We must realize that anyone who is capable of retaliating harshly is inherently empty of compassion. In particular, it is silly when people retaliate merely to force compassion in their relationships.

672. Love and anger are not compatible. Whoever uses anger to force (or keep) love is simply incapable of giving or taking love.

673. With the advent of various dating facilities, people meet and measure many candidates for dating. While this flexibility seems helpful to find a match, it increases people's false hopes about the possibility of finding a qualified person soon. Therefore, they become too fussy and keep joggling a bunch of relationships. Meanwhile, people who are truly suitable for being in relationships are becoming scarcer, too.

674. People keep multiple relationships, because they doubt the viability of any of them. In addition, it is more efficient to study a few potential partners simultaneously, as it usually takes many years to get to know someone even slightly. Multiple relationships can also help a person rebound faster if one of his/her favourite relationships fails. He/she has other relationships to lean on at least temporarily. All these justifications sound reasonable, but what a world we have created.

675. Our hopes to eventually find a soul mate is a naive incentive that stops us from making genuine efforts and commitments in a relationship or keeping our promises.

676. Under these tough circumstances, maybe the best definition for a soul mate is, 'Someone we can get along with rather peacefully, finally!'

677. Another cause of the increasing mistrust in relationships and society is that everybody is aware of the games people play, including multiple dating. Therefore, it is hard for people to take their courting and relationships seriously.

678. Oddly enough, though, everybody is also still too eager and hopeful to find a reliable companion, as if s/he would arrive from another planet. People's lasting struggle and optimism to find love, trust, and happiness are both admirable and disheartening. It is depressing, since people seem eager to dismiss the daunting realities of relationships in the new era.

679. Instead, people's reaction to new relationship conditions is just to do more of the same, i.e., more games, lying and mistrust, multiple dating, and more shallow relationships. Thus, the rising frustration and stress in society. Ironically, they still hope to succeed in finding a reliable companion and living happily ever after, too!

680. We have become a special (spoiled) generation—asking for more love while getting more arrogant every day. We do not realize that with more arrogance, we merely annihilate more of our patience and capacity to give and receive love.

681. Our children are getting even more spoiled in terms of their idealism, instead of appreciating, and preparing themselves for, life and relationships' hardships. Therefore, the dreadful trends in relationship failures would keep accelerating for coming generations.

682. Couples' knowledge of success factors for relationships is declining more every day.

683. Consequently, as a devastating trend in the new era, couples judge the health of their relationships arbitrarily or based on phony values, because no authentic criteria exist for setting practical standards and gauging the success of relationships.

684. Especially, partners still keep insisting on love and objects as the main success factors for relationships—the only tangible criteria they can think of, nowadays!

685. Couples have little patience and interest to learn about the basic problems of relationships in a serious manner, e.g., reading books like this one. At best, people have only time and patience for learning about some possible quick fixes, which have no ultimate value, anyway. People read those kinds of books or follow a few of counsellors' advices only to show that they did something to boost their relationships and still it did not work.

686. Meanwhile, relationship failures, ongoing clashes, and sad statistics keep raising mistrust among partners. Yet, people still ask for more love to justify their relationships, define

their lives, and find happiness. The big contrast is obvious when people insist on love while the overall trust is fading fast in society. Love in the absence of trust! How could couples really be sincere about their love expressions and exchanges when deep down, in their subconscious, their mistrusts about people, including their partners, linger?

687. It is hard to imagine that 'trust' can be rebuilt within society and relationships anytime soon and couples become largely convinced about it.

688. Therefore, while couples *pretend* to start their relationships based on trust, deep down they remain justifiably sceptical about it. This is true despite their convincing expressions of love and the roles they play mostly through MLove.

689. The meanings of love, lust, and trust have intermingled and become convoluted. This is causing additional mistrust and shakier social behaviour. All those casual sex with different partners, while talking about finding love, are not congruent values or plans. Satisfying our sexual drives is a practical choice in a modern society, but confusing it with love is hypocritical and impractical.

690. Overall, it is naïve to depend on 'love' or 'trust' to build a relationship. Instead, couples need objective mechanisms, principles, and a framework to map their marriages.

691. Couples are unaware of their personal flaws and how badly everybody gets damaged psychologically during their marital experiences. They believe in their purity, but also finding a perfect partner. Thus, they keep looking for some untenable ideal life that matches their fantasies.

692. In the older times, couples believed that marriage's most crucial goal was to share life's hardships. They knew how difficult life really was. They were ready and willing to make personal sacrifices and help each other sincerely. They played their angelic roles to reduce each other's burdens.

693. However, nowadays, many couples do just the opposite. For one thing, people are pushing themselves to stay positive

and believe that life is splendid and manageable. Therefore, instead of sharing life's hardships, they demand happiness and create more burdens for each other with a slight sign of inconvenience. Their naive expectations and dreams about marital life make them view any nuisance an unacceptable barrier in their relationships. And they rush to abandon their partners for greener pastures. Nowadays, marital objectives are mainly revolving around partners' obsessions for love, sexuality, and happiness.

694. There is a race in society to behave pompously, strive for a lot of things and compassion, and be highly competitive, all as a modern trend. Everybody also likes to appear highly sociable, pretentious, and popular. When people go to work on Mondays, they keep asking one another what they did on the weekend, as though measuring a person's completeness and worth.

695. Humans' inner conflicts are responsible for their confusion, stress, and sufferings in life, which affect their relationships, too, eventually.

696. At the same time, humans' *elementary* inner forces to be good are always in conflict with the external forces goading them to be bad. The modern society advocates arrogance, greed, hypocrisy, and dominance just to name a few of the crooked trends in the new era.

697. People have become calculating and opportunistic (users), due to their bad experiences and conditioning, including their conviction that life is too short and precious. They use various schemes to strengthen their positions and get ahead, and they associate mostly with those whom they find useful to them somehow. Then, this general perception (regarding people's hypocrisy, calculating nature, and insincerity) also affects relationships, as partners judge each other based on their shallow criteria of life, but also their overall mistrust.

698. How can people's romanticism be sincere when most of them try to be practical, too, (often by being so calculating

and materialistic) in such a chaotic environment? These are contradictory goals. Our social setting is destroying people's perceptions of one another and 'love'.

699. Couples are less capable, nowadays, to perceive and judge their relationships in its totality. They are readily influenced by their peculiar need urgencies and they are easily irritated by single events. The innate advantages of relationships are largely ignored due to couples' fast, egotistical judgments based on emotional episodes and erroneous perceptions.

Gender Driven Trends

700. The depth of relationship dilemmas (facts) noted in this book is horrendous already. However, the matter gets many folds more complicated due to the erratic ways that men and women perceive and deal with these relationship facts and dilemmas in the new era.

701. Relationship changes in the new era, e.g., the trend regarding people's drive for more independence, have affected women and men differently and raised more gender conflicts. Some of the prevalent emerging trends due to (or causing) gender differences are noted below.

702. A 'typical woman' image has been evolving in the new era mostly due to women's recent efforts to achieve equality, individualism, and independence. They have developed and portrayed a special role and identity for themselves. On the other hand, men have not yet tried to create and propagate an identity for themselves. They have not been active in projecting a picture of a typical man.

703. However, men are stereotyped as selfish and unromantic. In reality, however, men are simply lost and lack any identity, nowadays, because they have difficulty understanding and coping with women's new demands. Moreover, they have difficulty defining and asserting themselves at this time, which then leads to their further withdrawal or aggression.

704. Men and women are inherently incompatible in terms of their natural tendencies. Thus, partners' effort to find their compatible companion is mostly a shot in the dark already. Then, the new relationship approaches and games make the job of finding our soul mate many folds tougher.

705. The impressions that women and men make on one another by their attitudes, peculiar demands, and games are causing more distance between them. These games are too difficult to understand or absorb, and thus cause more inner conflicts for them according to their genders.

706. For example, the inner conflicts caused by less overall trust in relationships vs. more demands for love are felt deeper by men. This is mostly due to men's supposedly higher logical tendencies whereas women are more emotional and dynamic. With lower MLove and Model, men are usually handicapped in expressing love already, but when overall trust is low, the idea of expressing love becomes even more awkward for them.

707. On the other hand, women are more capable of expressing love, even when their trust is not high. This is due to their higher MLove and Model. Men lack this flexibility, while women have a hard time accepting this fact, and instead wonder why men are passive most often and not responding to their demand for attention as much as they like.

708. Sadly, the level of trust about our partners' words will keep declining and leads to more relationship failures. Therefore, expressing love with honesty will get even more difficult, especially for men.

709. Accordingly, men usually give up the possibility of finding a soul mate sooner than women do. They might look for a companion, nonetheless, but not with the aim of finding love. Women remain romantic and optimistic about finding a soul mate due to their higher intuitiveness and Model.

710. Women have been able to bond and support one another to set the rules of relationships. They are establishing a crude

culture that might eventually prove quite dysfunctional for maintaining relationships.

711. An advantage of women's bonding is that they get plenty of support when they leave their relationships. On the other hand, because of this bonding, and in line with the women's general attempt to propagate the new culture, they also goad one another to be least tolerant of their relationship flaws and abandon their spouses quickly.

712. Therefore, while women seem to help each other in terms of support after separation, they might also be sabotaging one another and causing more separations, *maybe intentionally even,* by provoking one another with their progressive ideas and attitude.

713. Men, on the other hand, do not have a sense of empathy, nor enough Model, to soothe each other's hurts once they leave their wives. Part of this deficiency is because men keep their emotions private to protect their pride. Women show their emotions but move on faster.

714. Women are emotionally stronger by nature, and due to their higher social adaptability and Model. This helps them in terms of rebounding quickly after separation. Then, their ability to support one another helps them recover even faster and better. Still, the same need for social adaptability and Model makes them anxious to find a new companion.

715. Women's intuitiveness, higher Model, and bonding ability give them more resilience and optimism about life and love, which help them adapt better to disappointments and social changes. Overall, they do not get too discouraged by their failures in past relationships. Yet, the number of women on anti-depressants is twice that of men.

716. Conversely, men usually take longer to heal their wounds and recommit themselves to another relationship, due to their lesser resilience and poor support after separation. This additional, long agony teaches them better lessons, which

ironically usually delay their urge for entertaining a serious relationship.

717. Men's logic and mistrust usually override their emotional needs, unlike women. Yet, their lower social adaptability makes them more vulnerable to submit to women's whims out of loneliness—but not necessarily out of love.

718. Pessimism about finding even a reliable companion, never mind a soul mate, has made men passive and this is making women frustrated, and more assertive.

719. Women do not seek men necessarily out of love, loneliness, or merely for the sake of having a companion. They already have many companions in other women. Satisfying their social and security needs often takes precedence over their craving for love or even companionship. This is true despite the emphasis made in the earlier notes about women's drive for love. Women's higher urge for social adaptation make them seek a partner to fit and feel better in social gatherings, to complete their identity, and for support. Higher maternal urges drive women, too, of course.

720. At the same time, ironically, most women believe in the likelihood of finding love and an ideal partner, compared with men who give up faster, thus seek a companion mostly out of loneliness and for satisfying their basic needs.

721. In fact, women appear to have a higher need and talent for all three levels of love, i.e., ELove, MLove, and Slove, than men. This aptitude pushes them to pursue love at any cost, but also get depressed deeper for failing.

722. Therefore, for women, both their higher social tendencies and neediness for love make them not only to believe in the possibility of finding a soul mate, but also more adamant to pursue this objective.

723. Conversely, men prefer some seclusion. Thus, their need for a companion is more for avoiding total loneliness. Men like socializing too, of course, but it is not their main motivation for finding a companion. Men socialize mostly to make

their wives happy, to come across sociable, or to stir variety in their lives.

724. Despite their urges for a companion and obsession to enjoy life at its fullest, too, more women than men give their kids' welfare a higher priority, even at the cost of postponing a serious relationship after a marriage breakdown until their children look relatively ready or independent. Accordingly, most women believe they deserve their kids' higher love, too, which they usually get more than fathers do.

725. Of course, many exceptions exist when women in particular go to all extremes to acquire or protect a new partner, even at the cost of hurting their children.

726. Fathers' traditional authority and respect has diminished in families for several reasons. **First,** women have assumed the ultimate role and responsibility for raising children and they perform this difficult task with power and decisiveness. Children observe their mothers in charge and their fathers passive with little role around the family. **Second,** mothers dedicate themselves to their kids more often than fathers do. Accordingly, children make a mental note of their mothers' devotion. They also feel a higher bond with their mothers instinctually the same way mothers feel towards their kids. **Third,** children see their mothers vulnerable and needy for attention, especially because women usually parade their vulnerability through Model shrewdly. Therefore, children feel obliged to take care of their mothers more than they see a need to sympathize with their fathers.

727. The bottomline is that men feel less involved with kids and not receiving enough love and respect. Their wives actually treat them a lot like another one of their kids, including an authoritative tone in their conversations with their husbands.

728. Nonetheless, the lower level of respect and power for sad fathers has made a negative impact on the wellbeing of the whole family.

729. The overall trend is that women are striving to create and express their new strong identity after decades of oppression by men. They have learned to be assertive and support one another to establish their individuality and identity. On the other hand, men are losing their individuality and identity due to the ambiguity of the gender roles and relationships' new atmosphere. This is an evolving picture overall, yet the ultimate outcome would be risky and questionable for both genders, but even more so for societies as a whole.

730. For one thing, women's success to enforce their new identity hinges a lot on men's reaction to their demands and the roles women expect them to play. More crucially, however, both men and women can truly attain, and feel comfortable with, their identities only with a reliable companion in their lives. Our everlasting, inherent urge to find our soul mates is the best indication of our sense of incompleteness (lack of identity) without a good companion. This book's discussions show that our need for a companion is an urgent and crucial need. It can potentially satisfy a large number of personal needs of humans stretching from the basic need for sex to the divine need for SLove. When these needs are unfulfilled, few humans might develop enough psychological security to affirm their gender identities in the new era.

731. Women may pretend to understand, and be happy with, their emerging identity. However, when they reflect on their lives sincerely, they notice that their new identity is incomplete and hurtful without a companion. Indeed, they need a man in their lives more than ever nowadays; more than men need a woman. This is due to women's higher Model and fervour for social activity.

732. Thus, women's identity is questionable without a man or if they are unhappy with their companion. For one thing, they remain too preoccupied with the task of finding their soul mates, due to their optimism about finding an ideal partner. As stated before, men are not so optimistic about finding a

soul mate and they are less obsessed about a companion (or even an identity) due to their lower Model.

733. Accordingly, as long as women's drive for identity reduces their chances of finding or keeping *competent* men, they would never find their genuine identity. 'Competent' refers to men with seeming strong characters (identity). No woman would enjoy a man with a weak character. A man without a strong identity is worthless even for women. Still, many women do not mind weakening their husbands' spirits.

734. A cynical observation about relationships in the new era is that sometimes women seek men mostly to exert their power over them, to prove their identity and superiority However, this strategy fails for the reasons noted above.

735. It is absurd that all these conflicting forces are somehow corrupting relationship environments. Men are confused and lost for the time being, anyway. However, their innate resistance and passivity are damaging women's attempt to assert their own identity. This is, in particular, true when the result is women's lesser access to *competent* men to support them mentally and physically.

736. Having emphasized enough on the fact that both genders need a companion to establish and exercise their identities, a more distressing fact must be stressed again as well. That is, even when they are in a relationship, neither gender can find its new identity because of their never-ending clashes.

737. Thus, genders' attempts to find their identities fail whether they are in a relationship or not, unless they adopt a more practical relationship framework to relate more effectively. The reason is that, while the conditions for creating personal identities are not pure and unselfish, partners continue to fight in order to enforce their perceptions of ideal identities for their genders.

738. In another word, partners' misperceptions of themselves and their partners, as well as their erroneous impression of ideal identities for their genders, prevent them from finding their

genuine, viable identities. Besides, their lasting clashes suck their energies to find and exert any kind of identity.

739. With no set identities, so many inner conflicts overwhelm both genders. Thus, when partners meet, they want to set the tone of their relationship by playing all kinds of games, in hopes of manipulating and controlling their relationship.

740. Two types of role-playing are becoming prevalent in new relationships with adverse effects, while widening gender differences and quarrels, too. First, the role-playing schemes that marriage counsellors advocate with the goal of stirring communication and love in relationships. This technique's weakness is that as long as partners do not grasp and resolve the roots of their relationship problems, playing roles only frustrates them. All the added superficial communications actually confuse them more and drive them away from the reality of their relationship. Instead, couples must somehow admit and tackle the main sources of their conflicts directly.

The second type of role-playing hurts relationships even more. It begins from the minute partners meet and continues throughout their relationship. Couples play all kinds of roles and games to impress, manipulate, confuse, lure, or deceive each other. They exaggerate or lie in all respects in order to control the situation and succeed: by flattering, getting too emotional, showing apathy, proving their independence and power, retaliating, and so many other games that continue throughout the dating process and in their relationship, too.

741. Couples' goal for playing so many roles is to set precedence in their relationships and enforce their needs. They strive to establish their authorities and territories from the beginning around certain boundaries. Thus, it is becoming impossible to sense people's true personalities and sincerity, nowadays. Role-playing (including retaliations or reactions, as defence mechanisms) might be somewhat justified since everybody gets hurt in relationships at some point. Couples play games to prevent more headaches. But, then, they lose the chance

of relaxing, being natural, and building a calm and effective relationship.

742. By playing games, people have also minimized their level of objectivity as well as their partners'. Thus, they suffer, while their relationships also follow a destructive course. Role-playing (phoniness) also lowers couples' opportunities of finding companions who might appreciate them for who they really are. Instead, they only struggle with both their own phony personalities (to appear convincing and natural), and their partners' (to understand them perhaps).

743. While most people like to rely on their clever Model to play appealing roles for attracting love and sympathy, they try to hide their strong Ego and haughtiness behind Model. In a society where arrogance has become such a dominant social attribute, even Model promotes pomposity. Therefore, it is getting difficult to understand who a person really is behind so much show of self-importance.

744. Women are becoming more active socially and placing a high value on living a materialistic life to its fullest. They need to do more things, go to various functions, and travel extensively, all in hopes of finding that elusive happiness. At the same time, men are becoming more passive, content, and couch potatoes.

745. Overall, it is fair to say that women are the stronger gender now. Congratulations!

746. Nowadays, men are the weaker gender in terms of emotional vulnerability (personality), despite the fact that women are more emotional. The reasons for this seeming contradiction are explained in this chapter. Actually, men's weakness is widely known and propagated regularly in the new era. Even advertising agencies exploit this perception whenever they can benefit from it (see note 765 below).

747. Women are also quite aware of men's vulnerability. Thus, it feels natural to them to exploit this loophole to push their ideologies and obtain everything they believe they deserve.

748. Due to their higher reliance on intuition, decisiveness, and the teachings of the new culture, women are trying to be in charge of the family. They seem to be good at it, too, in many respects. However, in the process, they also feel the need to prove their superiority to men. Well, since women are the stronger gender in reality, why should not they be in charge or try to show off their superiority occasionally? The problem is that superiority by either gender cannot work in the new era where the emphasis must be placed on equity, individualism, independence, and satisfying personal needs and ambitions.

749. Therefore, women's attempt to prove their superiority leads to further deterioration of relationships and more mistrust. Of course, some husbands prefer to be quite passive and/or submissive. Many women actually do not mind turning their husbands into submissive men in order to feed their own Ego and ELove. Some women might think, "Why not give it a try, anyway, and see if it works." However, in the end, this situation cannot prevail in progressive societies.

750. Relationships would go through a lengthy, erratic transition period while women try to assert themselves and find their identity. It would be a harsh and frustrating process because their present approach is both impractical and illogical.

751. During this transitional period, women have difficulty being a modest (content) wife in an environment that advocates a domineering attitude to enforce equality and identity. Many women have been successful in practising this approach in their relationships already. They present very appealing role models for the rest of them. Women's influence over one another is too strong to be ignored, by either women or men. Mothers, daughters, female colleagues and friends are placing lots of pressure on one another, nowadays, to behave assertively. Any woman who attempts to behave differently might be ousted. Yet, more importantly, she would feel sad for not being a typical (assertive) woman like others.

752. It is quite likely that many men have become passive and submissive, since they are less capable of bonding together, thus becoming the weaker gender. Moreover, men are less eager to define and maintain a strong identity. Their logical minds, passivity, ambitions, and neediness for a companion are keeping them the weaker gender they have most likely always been.

753. Men's resort to violence and physical domination are good clues indeed about their inability to keep up with the kind of games that women are better at playing so naturally. Men's frustration is also due to their inability to keep up with women's needs, which men often find illogical, anyway.

754. Women seem to be winning most battles in relationships, but it is doubtful that any gender can win the big war that is going on. The point is that, as long as one gender or one partner is weaker than the other, their relationship remains dysfunctional. Not enough respect or challenge remains for either partner (mainly the stronger) to take their relationship serious or stay in it. This fact is indeed most relevant in our new culture where individualism and self-esteem have found such high values.

755. Therefore, women's urge to establish their superiority in the new era would not benefit anybody in the end. Women are behaving naturally, of course, according to their inherent personality strengths and huge bonding capability. Yet, their efforts are already putting relationships in great jeopardy. They would be the ones suffering the repercussions of the existing situation the most, because they are more sensitive and they believe in love.

756. Surely, relationships get into trouble because both partners are at fault in some respects. And because the whole society has lost control over both the economy and relationship norms. Even when a partner is smart, patient, and humble to make the relationship work, the chances of saving his/her relationship are still low. The reason is that his/her modest

behaviour is perceived as a sign of weakness, instead of goodness. He/she is treated poorly or ignored. Thus, both partners are normally forced to be assertive, which usually turns into aggressiveness and quarrels.

757. The emerging relationship dilemmas resemble the global warming mayhem. Nobody is willing to admit the existence of a fundamental problem or do anything about it. The main reason, also like global warming, is the economy and greed. Materialism and hypocrisy would not let partners become more realistic about their approaches and social values, which they have adopted rather naively.

758. Women go into their next relationships with even higher expectations, instead of less. They believe that their reasons for leaving their past relationships (such as need for more compassion or love) had been justified, therefore their new relationships must make up for everything they had missed before. They want to prove to themselves and others that leaving their previous partners had been good decisions. Therefore, they look for more love, luxury, and security.

759. Conversely, men usually set lower expectations and prepare themselves for less authority if they get into another serious relationship.

760. An effect of women's intuitiveness is that their priorities somewhat change quickly after having their children. For one thing, they are forced to exercise a lot of authority to make their children follow their rules. A mother is driven instinctually to manage her life as well as her children's. Therefore, she becomes authoritative, commanding, and demanding. These are mostly instinctual traits that surface when her life begins to get hectic with children and maybe a lazy husband—maybe even testing her patience! She also finds less time for her husband after children are born. He suddenly gets a lower priority and importance, maybe not intentionally but rather practically. Furthermore, she learns soon that it is more efficient and natural to treat her husband

like another one of her children. She must organize things and manage family affairs the way she has found productive through her child-rearing experiences. Her tactics, such as commanding, demanding, and impatience, feel most natural and effective to her for running the family affair.

761. For men, however, their wives' gradual (but drastic) change feels unnatural and annoying eventually. They attribute it to their wives' loss of interest and romance. In this confusing environment, women look rather insensitive, impatient, and sometimes even cruel, in the way they run the household, including their husbands, so rigidly.

762. Overall, women's decisiveness goads them to play a stricter role in building relationship settings and imposing the rules.

763. Men, on the other hand, are lazy to argue or fuss too much. Thus, more women are becoming in charge of the family, while men are becoming more submissive.

764. Accordingly, most partners, especially men, learn to stay somewhat passive in order to cope with their substandard relationship situation.

765. The existing culture hinders teamwork. Actually, an image of men's submissiveness (and maybe their idiocy) is often propagated even in TV commercials to sell products to women. For example, while writing this chapter, a couple of TV commercials caught the author's eyes. They reflect how idiotically social and relationship trends are perceived and exploited even by advertisers:

The first commercial was about Multigrain Cheerios. The box apparently refers to 120 calories per serving. The husband makes an innocent comment to his wife: "Are you trying to watch your diet?"

"Do I look like I need to watch my diet?" the wife asks with irritation and sarcasm.

"No, honey, I'm just stating what the box says (about its low calories)," the poor husband replies with a guilty tone in absolute panic.

"What else the box says?" the wife demands.

"The box says, 'Shut up, Steve,'" the husband replies with shame and misery. The wife smirks.

The second commercial was about McCain's Deep and Delicious frozen cake. The wife is enjoying the cake. And the husband is trying to get his wife's attention and support about his dream of becoming a mime. However, she is not paying attention to his comments and enactment of some miming gestures, because she is supposedly absorbed by the taste of the cake. When she notices him at last, she demands with impatience, "What're you doing?"

The husband freezes in his miming gesture like a lamb facing a lion suddenly. "I'm living my dream," he replies with total panic and desperation again.

"Stop it," the wife orders him.

The husband stops, scared stiff and mute like an idiot. The commercial ends. The wife makes the ruling and that is the end of the story for the humiliated husband who likes to live his dream of becoming a mime.

Humour is allegedly the intention of these commercials, to sell their products. Yet, they are recklessly propagating women's assertiveness and men's passivity and pathetic subordination in relationships in the new era—, which is largely true but not a proper viewpoint. They exploit the fact that men are put down by women and they cannot do a darn thing about it. They advocate women's power, all for the sake of flattering and goading them to buy their products.

766. These commercials reflect the reality of relationships, but also propagate arrogance. They find it funny that women's superiority is becoming a big trend and part of our emerging culture, including aggression towards men. But, 'How and when are we going to convince ourselves that these values are destructive for both genders? How many more centuries before we are convinced? Maybe ten is a good guess!

767. If someone asks the author to identify the most destructive force ruining relationships, 'Hollywood' is a good answer. Those naïve love stories, senseless gender confrontations, and meaningless conclusions have been infecting the brains of the public all over the world. Some ignorant writers are doing everybody a disservice by their unrealistic, simple-minded scripts. A scene in the movie *Two Weeks Notice* with Sandra Bullock and Hugh Grant is really confusing and interesting: Sometime in the middle of the night, Sandra is returning a pair of shoes that she had borrowed from her friend—a weird timing all by itself. After the friend goes down and opens the door, they sit down near the curb to talk. The friend's husband appears at the window of their apartment, looks down into the street with concern, and asks with confusion, "Everything's okay?" The wife yells at him with attitude, "Not now! Everything is not about you!" Her comment and tone of voice has no relevance and meaning in that scene or in the context of the whole movie. It only reflects the absurdity of relationships' atmosphere.

"Okay," the husband mumbles with apprehension as he moves away from the window pitifully. Naturally, he would have most likely been accused of apathy if he had not tried to find out if his wife were okay, because all he knew was that she had gone downstairs to answer the door that late at night.

768. Women's higher intuition leads to other hurdles, too. First, it makes them hasty and dogmatic in their views. Second, it raises their tendency to see, feel, and judge things without enough contemplation and communication. Often they even believe they can somehow read their husbands' minds and detect the hidden clues in their comments. They also assume that men have the same level of intuition to understand their wives' wishes without communicating the ideas to them

clearly. They say something and expect their husbands to read between the lines and understand their intentions. Then, they get surprised and frustrated when their husbands do not comprehend their messages. In fact, they often believe that their husbands have gotten the message, but are refusing to accept it or do something about it. Women believe that men are (or should be) as careful and intuitive as they are. They do not recognize that men's lower intuitiveness cannot be helped. Besides, men's crude logic rules their need for clear communication, instead of guessing the meaning of a vague message.

769. Overall, women do not believe in, and actually resist, an open and detailed communication, maybe because they feel their husbands are not listening or interested, anyway. Yet, women have also become oversensitive and react harshly when men cannot understand their vague messages. As noted above, women's intuition is filling the gap that hinders men's grasp of a message without full communication. Men need clarity and women resist it, as they find it unnecessary and unromantic; or stay vague out of spite occasionally, too. They just expect their husbands to grasp their meanings and intentions. For example, a husband was complaining to the author that whenever his wife realized her mistake, she only tried to make up for it by making his favourite meal, buying him a pair of socks, or making an indirect gesture of these natures. However, she never apologized directly or admitted a mistake. She simply expected to get the matter resolved quickly (swept under the rug) without acknowledging the problem or discussing it. He complained that, without an open discussion about the problem and a sincere apology, the matter never got resolved in his mind and his wounds never healed. Actually, he considered his wife's behaviour (the gesture of buying him a present or cooking a fine meal) another type of manipulation and her rising arrogance.

770. As a new trend, couples usually misjudge the hurdles of finding a new companion after getting out of their existing relationships. They are naïve and too optimistic about their chances of finding a good match, even in their older ages. This is in particular difficult for women who are seeking men of higher qualities after their past relationships fail. Thus, couples' problems and frustrations would keep rising in their second and third relationships, unless one or both partners become rather passive after realizing the depth and prevalence of relationship obstacles, nowadays.

771. Many smart couples, however, learn to perceive and handle their relationships more practically, despite all the forces in society to make them radical in their relationships. These couples prefer to handle the imperfections of their present relationships patiently, rather than following the trend to seek a new relationship, which often has inevitable flaws of its own. They simply get used to the conflicts and their partners' shortfalls after many years of sharing both good memories and life's hardships together. They learn to bear their relationship flaws by always recalling its merits. They admit that both partners in almost all relationships are most likely annoyed by each other's idiosyncrasies. They feel that bearing the imperfections of their existing relationship is easier than learning about, and accepting, a stranger's (a new companion's) imperfections all of a sudden. Men are particularly lazy, too, to go through the hassle of finding a new companion if the existing relationship is still bearable.

772. People expect peace in a new relationship after bearing their last partners' flaws. Especially for men, staying lonely feels preferable to living with a person who brings a new set of idiosyncrasies and childish demands. Learning new stuff and adjusting, especially at older ages, is taxing. With old age, we need less sex and have less patience or incentives, anyway, while getting grouchy and demanding, too.

More Behavioural Trends (causing deep gender conflicts)

773. Everybody, especially women, is getting more sensitive and defensive in his/her interactions due to his/her controversial past relationships and the rising level of aggressiveness in society. Naturally, this trend stirs additional psychological pressures in relationships. We speak with people and our partners with caution (superficially) to avoid triggering their defence mechanisms and starting arguments. This situation keeps relationships too edgy and unnatural.

774. Still, while trying to appear tactful and calm, people are also getting more aggressive and offensive to offset other people or their partners' assertiveness; as the old saying goes: The best defence is offence.

775. Often relationships get messy when partners are unhappy with themselves and their lives, thus depress their partners with their attitudes, too. They blame their partners for their own unhappiness, career failures, boredom, or unfulfilled dreams. Sometimes, they nag at each other to conceal their own shortfalls, for example, in socializing. Then, they hate each other gradually, since they believe their partners are actually responsible for their unhappiness. Does this attitude apply more to one gender?!

776. Partners waste a lot of time and energy on faultfinding and blaming each other, nowadays, supposedly for improving their relationship. If only they realized that, in the end, it does not matter whose fault the problems are as long as they remain irreconcilable and disastrous!

777. The bottomline is that couples should either find mutually agreeable solutions (a suitable relationship model) to relate somehow or separate. While the present trend is towards the latter, the former feels more natural and productive.

778. When relationship problems go beyond certain point, the only solution is to find ways of relating (living together) passively at a lower level of the 'relationship needs tree' (model), and stop trying to solve the problems per se.

779. Relationship problems are often unsolvable, since they are caused by partners' irreversible idiosyncrasies. We arrogant humans have proven that not even our alleged intelligence and logic can help us solve our personal or socioeconomic problems.

780. Gender struggles to reach some illusory balance of power and equality is continuing at many levels, and the situation will most likely get out of hand soon with global destructive outcomes.

781. We have difficulty learning from our mistakes and from the pains that our relationships are causing us. We prefer to hurt one another and suffer personally than change our attitude about the inherent limitations of relationships, especially within the context of the existing lifestyles.

782. Accordingly, it would be hard for the contentious messages of this book to find popularity amidst the mass of artfully packaged messages (and social values) promising prosperity and happiness to everybody.

783. One of the main objectives of a relationship framework is to bring *objectivity* back into relationships. However, a main hurdle is selling the idea of objectivity to women who are used to dealing with issues intuitively, and to men whose crude sense of logic has already made them too dogmatic.

784. Nonetheless, society must gradually promote the guidelines of a relationship framework. A logical atmosphere should replace gender struggles for superiority. Reaching a balance of power and identity requires some level of objectivity soon. Otherwise, present relationship trends would cause more chaos for societies and families.

785. A puzzling point is, 'What kind of partners are couples looking for when they insist on breaking each other's pride and spirit, mainly by competing with each other non-stop?' In particular, a relevant question is, "Whether women can ever find submissive men attractive and trustworthy at all?" How could women enjoy or respect weak men?

786. Another major conflict is emerging: Couples are expecting their partners to be strong, forceful, and assertive outside the house to maximize families' welfare, but be submissive and passive at home to accommodate them.

787. The emerging social trends, especially couples' needs for individuality and independence, are irreversible. People's psychological attributes and urges due to gender differences cannot be changed, either. Therefore, the only solution for our relationships is to find new mechanisms and principles to match our new needs.

788. In addition, couples must get more serious about modifying their mindsets and viewing relationships in a more practical perspective. They should do so for increasing their chances of building a reliable relationship. A productive relationship environment must be envisioned and propagated.

789. Partners' urges for individualism alienate them. However, working within a progressive relationship framework solves this problem largely, as partners' independence and rational individualism get priority. Couples learn to respect and face their partners' need for independence, and actually perceive 'independence' as a requirement of teamwork. All along, detailed mechanisms of teamwork can be developed and practised as well.

790. The irony is that hardly can anybody find his or her soul mate merely due to the way we behave, nowadays. Even if we happen to find them by accident, we just keep losing them due to our phony personalities and ideologies, not to mention our idiotic games and egos. It is bizarre that even couples with similar values, lifestyle, and priorities reject one another merely because they do not know how to relate effectively and naturally—mainly because they do not know how to choose a proper relationship model.

791. Some couples have indeed found their soul mates, but they lose them when their own oversensitivity gives them wrong impressions about the health of their relationship and the

purpose of relationships in general. They lose their partners due to their fantasies, such as a better life with a different partner, love, money, etc. Couple's misperceptions and high expectations are making them lose the soul mates they have already found.

792. Partners get too intimate too early as a sign of love, trust, and loyalty, instead of proving all of these high qualities gradually through real actions and right attitude. Often, partners actually try to manipulate each other by showing off a polished image of themselves. Nevertheless, statistics show that most couples end up losing their love, trust, and loyalty in their relationships.

793. We seek relationships to relieve our loneliness, but realize the absurdity of our dreams fast, since relationships actually make us feel the ultimate depth of loneliness and despair.

794. Partners try to exploit each other (knowingly or naively) by *activating their MLove to fake SLove to get ELove.*

795. People assume they are (or can be) loving, trustworthy, or loyal. However, all emerging trends and evidences indicate that humans are impure by nature, and then environment makes them even more cruel and aggressive.

796. Relationships suffer from humans' inherent defects more than anything else. Some artificial expressions of passion, due to attraction or other needs of partners, do not change their true nature as humans with all their inherent defects.

797. Our rampant relationship issues are causing more mistrust amongst youth. Therefore, each generation is causing more damages for the relationships of the future generations. We are making our children more sceptical about marriage and less prepared to handle its requirements, especially its most likely consequence, i.e., separation.

798. Driven by the recent popular ideologies, including 'positive thinking' slogans, people like to believe that life is beautiful and happiness is within reach. Yet, prominent philosophies and our personal experiences indicate the opposite: That life

is nothing but a place for suffering and paying for our past or present sins. The point is that our idealism and search for this phantom happiness are misleading many couples; they just put too much demand on each other recklessly before finally separate.

799. It is a pity that our misguided perceptions prevent us from taking advantage of our only opportunity to suffer less in this world—by bringing objectivity into our relationships and enjoying one another, instead of arguing so much about our inconsequential needs and crude obsessions, especially this illusive 'happiness.' We are proving the philosophers right, in fact, about life being only a place for suffering. For one thing, we suffer from our relationships (or lack of them) due to our own naïve expectations and games.

800. Being optimistic and positive about life are useful tools. However, when they cause gross misperceptions and raise our naïve expectations, e.g., for more love or compassion, they must be seen as another source of partners' confusion and relationship failures.

801. The bottomline is that if positive thinking and 'living in the now' schemes worked, everybody would have benefited from these magical cures by now and we could see all those bright faces around us. Relationship problems would have disappeared and everybody would have been living happily with their soul mates.

802. Yet, all we see is more depressions, addictions, neediness, suicides, personal failures, divorces, desperation, unrealistic expectations, and self-pity, nowadays. Antidepressants are the highest used drug in society (in the U.S. in particular) to help us continue living and suffering.

803. Many people are edgy these days, because their positive thinking alone, even when they mix it with lots of personal efforts, does not seem to help them. They still lose their mates to shoddy life philosophies that only mislead people,

and they still lose their life savings in financial markets due to other people's incompetence or greed.

804. Many philosophers believe life cannot be a happy affair, since the minute we have nothing to do, and can supposedly enjoy life, we get bored. Thus, we look for adventure, work, or a new companion to rejuvenate our lives. Yet, all these expected remedies make us suffer, too.

805. In all, we struggle all our lives to find something creative to do or a worthy mate to give us some moments of happiness. Some spiritualists believe we can get the best sense of this elusive happiness by learning to be better human beings and staying content, which is a tough mission for most of us.

806. Ironically, however, being a good human does not always pay off, nowadays. It might not help (or hurt in fact) his/her relationships, especially, if his/her spouse is not an equally good human. Thus, being a good person might not be useful necessarily for drawing other people's compassion or getting tangible benefits. Instead, he/she is often perceived as a weak and passive individual and not taken seriously.

807. Still, being good can at least mitigate our sufferings and possibly bring us peace and divinity, plus a better chance to relate to our partners unselfishly. This is a grand incentive, though, if we learn to be a bit wiser through self-awareness.

PART III

Relationship Choices

Chapter Twelve
Relationship Solutions

The facts and trends discussed in Parts I and II about the nature of relationships in the 21st century show that we have **three general choices**:

A. **Continue with the status quo**, hoping that nature will take its course and eventually a format for relationships will emerge. Meanwhile, there will be more separations, conflicts, and paranoia about relationships. And there is no way to predict the outcome. The chance that a logical and efficient framework evolves out of this chaos is slim.
B. **Hope that one gender will eventually dominate the other** so that order might return to relationships. It is a fact that humans have difficulty relating to one another and working as a team consistently, especially the opposite sexes. This is truer now with individualism, arrogance, and greed running our mindsets and social values. On the other hand, the option of one gender taking the superior role would not work in the end, either. Chaos and equality struggles would keep overwhelming relationships.
C. **Create and propagate a relationship framework** based on prevalent social mentalities to guide couples run their marriages smoothly and relate efficiently. With the rising complexity of societies, relationships' longevity appears

doomed, anyway. Yet, a flexible, modern relationship framework can at least do two things: 1) prepare couples for the high chance of relationship failures in the new era, and 2) reduce the level of frictions between couples.

808. Let us hope the third option appeals to most of us and we decide to support it actively, as only this option has a chance to bring some level of objectivity back into relationships. It will minimize partners' frictions and anguish, while also improve social life vastly. Moreover, couples will be better prepared to face the reality of separation and living alone independently. Nonetheless, this book advocates the third option, as it appears like the only solution.

809. We must also study the dozen **facts** outlines at the end of Chapter One (and reiterated below, too) and ponder our choices wisely. We can do something about these facts now or wait until relationships become totally unmanageable. The bottomline is that we have only limited choices to make our marriages somewhat more bearable before it is too late. The **bottomline** is that we must:

A: Upgrade our mindsets and acknowledge that:

- Both our initial optimism about relationships (when we start one) and subsequent retaliations (when it fails) are destructive.
- Our perspective of relationships is naïve, unrealistic, and incompatible with the format of modern societies. We must learn to lower our expectations from relationships to attend to our increasing personal needs independently.
- We must prepare ourselves, emotionally and financially, to deal with the high chance of failure in our marriages and relationships.
- Only by conscious efforts and major personal sacrifices, a relationship might survive. Our present mindsets (personal priorities) and social values make the job of prolonging our relationships difficult, if not impossible altogether.

B. Understand human limitations and accept the facts that:

- The complexity of human cognition and behaviour, driven by so many personal needs, perceptions, and traits, causes all kinds of relationship problems.
- The underlying causes of relationship failures are beyond partners' normal control. Overall, they cannot understand the causes of relationships' conflicts, elude their personal insecurities and flaws, or change themselves easily and quickly. Human's psychological defects and genetic built are making us all helpless.
- Our faultfinding attitude towards our partners is a futile exercise. Furthermore, our persistence to change others (including our partners) is absurd, especially when the matter is pursued through retaliation and intimidation.

C. Develop new relationship mechanisms and guidelines mainly by admitting that:

- Dynamic relationship principles are needed to reflect the realities of the modern world, especially people's rising obsessions for independence, individuality, and sexuality.
- New guidelines are needed to facilitate individuals' drive to be successful, assertive, proactive, and make the best use of their lives.
- Revolutionary social mechanisms and norms are needed to help us manage our relationships and possibly reduce their chances of failure.
- Dynamic social mechanisms and education (especially at high school) are needed to prepare couples for the reality of relationships, nowadays, especially separation and its related psychological effects.
- Radical laws should be devised to make separations easy and stress free.

810. Thus, as main mental adjustments, couples should:

a) Reduce their expectations from relationships drastically.

b) View relationships a temporary arrangement, unless they do all the right things (which would be rather unlikely for most people).
c) Know relationships' specific needs* before entering their relationships, and be mentally equipped and willing to observe these relationship needs and guidelines.
d) Learn, and be willing, to relate to each other within the boundaries of the relationship framework*. They should identify the relationship model that best fits their personal needs and personalities*.
e) Be prepared to leave their relationships with open mind, without fuss or retaliation and before they start to hate each other.
f) View their relationship as an independent entity like a business (romantic) enterprise. The concept of R-entity.
g) Not look up to the government to resolve their squabbles. Rather, they should depend on their initial contracts that outline their commitments to one another at the outset.
h) Remember that love, ethics, and religion are not reliable mechanisms to authenticate or protect relationships. The vows they exchange in those settings are good only for glamorizing their feelings and ceremonies.

811. In line with the required mental adjustments noted above, we have to make many tough choices mostly in terms of seeing relationships in a more progressive and realistic light.

---

* Discussing the following topics' details is beyond this book's scope:

- Relationship Needs
- Relationship Framework
- Relationship Models
- Relationship Expectations
- Relationship Guidelines
- Relationship Success Factors

Interested readers are encouraged to read about them in *The Nature of Love and Relationships* or in the *Relationship Needs, Framework, and Models,* (See the list of the author's book).

812. Relationship problems are too complex and widespread to overcome quickly. However, most frustrating and unsettling is our reluctance to acknowledge that this pandemic has deep roots and requires radical changes. With this kind of passive mindset, we are not making serious, systematic efforts to explore the underlying hurdles of relationships.

813. In fact, merely our passivity regarding the rising chaos and complexity of relationships is the main reasons why it will take at least a century, if at all, to find plausible solutions for them. Then again, we can improve our marriages personally today by making some minor changes in our mentalities.

814. Surely, making many tough choices outside the box, often against our egos and social norms, would not be easy, but we have no other option. That is precisely why revamping our mindsets about relationships is the most important task for humans after understanding the bottomline and our real choices enumerated in Part III.

815. For one thing, a big misperception in society and people's minds is that relationships must last forever. This traditional mentality and naïve expectation is misleading couples from the start when they weigh their choices. So romantically, we see relationships as a manageable and reliable arrangement that can fulfil many of our personal and relationship needs. Yet, the chance of any relationship failing is much higher than succeeding these days.

816. Nowadays, permanence is the least likely scenario going by the statistics on divorce, family problems, people's craze for individualism, sexuality, and the growing level of stress in society. Now, relationships are emerging with full force as an open-ended arrangement rather than a long-term, reliable commitment.

817. Thus, as a good start for adjusting our mentalities, we must now suddenly see marriages as *a temporary arrangement*, unless we are smart and lucky enough to make it work on a long-term basis. We must ponder this vital choice seriously.

818. Now couples must be able to play a special role and prove that they deserve to stay in their relationships. They carry a high burden of responsibility (by demonstrating their will and aptitude) for prolonging their relationships beyond the initial romantic era and as partners' patience begins to falter.

819. Naturally, this condition (to view relationships a temporary arrangement) appears like a big setback about relationships' success and value. The readers might ask, "How could this *seemingly* negative view help the success of relationships?" The answer is that, 'For solving relationships dilemmas, we must face reality somehow.' This awakening would actually help the state of relationships vastly, as explained in the next point.

820. In the author's opinion, we should indeed look forward very keenly to implement this progressive mindset and approach about the high vulnerability of relationships. The reason is that the advantages of such a mindset might amaze us in the end. This would prove to be one of those unique instances where 'reverse psychology' would prove to work extremely well. The couples' knowledge that their relationship would terminate *automatically* at a certain point would make them stay together much longer than would be under the present circumstance. They simply remain vigilant and protect their relationship in a constructive, teamwork environment. They realize that they should work on their relationship regularly, instead of taking it for granted and letting it end at a preset date. This reverse psychology would definitely reshape our mindsets and societies in at least four ways:

- Couples get into their relationships more carefully based on intelligent analyses of their needs, their compatibility, and a particular relationship model's suitability for them.
- Couples work harder and more consciously to prolong their relationships, instead of letting it expire. This would most likely increase the longevity of most relationships that are worth saving.

- Couples are mentally prepared to leave their relationships with the least amount of shock and hassle when it is not working. They know at the outset that separation is a good and acceptable possibility, if necessary.
- Ending relationships is automatic and hassle free.

821. Nevertheless, making such a harsh mental adjustment—to view relationships as a temporary arrangement—would be difficult for people. Therefore, it will take time to get there.
822. At the same time, people's present attitude indicates that they somehow handle their marriages like a temporary deal, anyway. Partners seem eager to abandon their relationships if their tough expectations are not met and they do not feel happy according to their demanding and calculating minds.
823. Although the longevity of relationships has many benefits if it can be properly mastered, three main questions remain:

- Are humans instinctually equipped to live together for the length of their lives (especially now that life expectancy is increasing so drastically)?
- Do partners' erratic personalities and needs support the possibility of living together forever?
- Do our new social values and settings promote the idea and possibility of relationship longevity?

824. The author explains and argues in his book, *The Nature of Love and Relationships* that the answer to all the three above questions is no.
825. One clue that humans are not instinctually programmed to live together permanently is their amazing zeal for sexual freedom. The urge to experience sex with many partners is in almost all human beings. As a means of happiness or psychological remedy, sex has also become too important for us to remain content with only one partner. Furthermore, sex is the first refuge we seek when our relationships face a calamity.

826. Another hurdle for relationship longevity is humans' innate difficulty to get along, especially the opposite sexes.

827. Discussions in Chapter Five about human hormones also show humans' low capacity and motivation for monogamy.

828. In all, it seems that humans are inherently not made to be in lasting relationships.

829. A good portion of people has even less capacity (including patience) to be in relationships due to their self-centredness and deep idiosyncrasies. Yet, we all try to force the idea of longevity out of habit, loneliness, urge for procreation, etc.

830. Nevertheless, couples' mental adjustment is necessary for all the reasons discussed in this book. One main objective is to make people more conscious and careful about the true nature of relationships in the new era. They must get more realistic and view relationships with open eyes and minds—not by the ways they feel and hope for. Most people are in fact doing this already, though in an incomplete way. They assess the financial prospects of their relationships furtively, but do not wish to admit its importance or express it openly. They try to avoid the accusation of being calculating and unromantic when they are starting a relationship. Anyway, we must act according to the statistics and vivid experiences around us.

831. We must admit to relationships' low longevity, nowadays, openly and prepare ourselves (financially and emotionally) for viewing relationships a temporary arrangement. Surely, the concept might appear too radical, if not vulgar, and it may turn off many readers already. Yet, considering all the facts, trends, and choices discussed in this book, the readers may feel supportive of the need for a progressive mentality and other radical suggestions offered in Chapter Fourteen.

832. Surely, it is unromantic and depressing to start relationships on a seemingly wrong foot and negative attitude. However, being realistic at the outset might save us time, separation hassles, and nervous breakdowns.

833. The challenges of separation seem inevitable for a majority of relationships and it pays off to be prepared for them.

834. Studying the roots of relationship failures would also help us realize they are merely the symptoms of social changes we have adopted hastily—such as stress on feminism—without grasping their personal and family implications or how to adapt ourselves to them. Thus, partners' retaliations out of spite cannot correct anything. It is just an awful, vain strategy in relationships. Retaliating to make our partners change is not going to work, either. It merely reflects our own utmost immaturity and wishful thinking.

835. As noted before, one objective of this book is to pinpoint the high vulnerability of relationships in modern societies. Low longevity is one of its obvious vulnerabilities. Still, with a realistic perception about this most likely outcome of relationships, we would have a more rational state of mind, make better choices when everything start going wrong, and react more constructively. At the same time, this boosted awareness might actually stir enough incentives and sincere efforts by us to save our relationships.

836. Learning about the inherent causes of relationship problems might help those who are smart and humble to take on a constructive role for managing their relationships. Adopting some relationship principles, as suggested in this book, is also for the same purpose, i.e., to make couples relate more effectively.

837. Understanding the complexity of human behaviour and its adverse effects on their relationships is the only remedy left to save couples. We must revamp our views of relationships, redefine our expectations realistically, and be prepared for the worst scenario, i.e., separation.

Appendix 12-A
Personality Aspects' Role

A potent solution for our ailing relationships is to learn about, monitor, and apply our personality aspects (Ego, Model, and Self) more actively and effectively. We have many choices in terms of understanding and using our personality aspects more effectively to help our relationships.

838. We can make a habit of monitoring and distinguishing the personality aspects in our encounters. We can be the best judge as to which one of them is in control during an event or communication. We sometimes do this assessment later after a conversation or event. Sometimes we feel sorry for what we had said. We might go back and try to correct our past mistakes at least. Usually, however, Ego stops us even from correcting our mistakes, i.e., by apologizing at least.

839. Especially, we can make an effort to use Self more often to soothe someone's hurt feelings. We know how to do this and probably do it occasionally. Therefore, it is possible to use Self more often if we just push ourselves to be a little more conscious of the personality aspect that is trying to dominate a message or action. In particular, we can assess the tone and content of our messages in advance.

840. After we do this simple exercise for a while, our awareness level enhances gradually, which then helps us further to gauge and improve our habits and attain the tranquility we crave all our lives. Of course, changing our personality and habits is not a straightforward matter. It does not occur fast or easily. Still, the mere sense of initiating a self-awareness regimen is crucial for overcoming the challenge of changing ourselves and perhaps the people around us. Keeping track of the interworking and manifestation of one's personality aspects is the most important step towards self-awareness.

841. Committing oneself to such a noble regimen is hard, as we must keep fighting our Egos without any tangible incentive. Attaining tranquility is the only incentive for self-awareness and personality change. This is a major incentive, though, if we really wish to find peace and happiness. This is the best way to acquire and enjoy a sense of relative freedom from social burdens and may even start to enjoy our relationships.

842. Obviously, breaking the rules of social belonging to build Self feels too naïve and ridiculous. How can we ignore the tangible rewards of social compliance like wealth, sex, and power, all in hopes of tranquility and freedom? These states appear to be abstract concepts and wishful thinking after all. For all these reasons, a person must feel the need to change his/her life's direction, and then gain the needed courage and commitment for pursuing the path of self-awareness. Some people reach this wisdom when they face life hurdles and hit the tall wall of disappointments, in particular in their relationships. Even then, they still require special insight to appreciate the need for an alternative lifestyle. Only this wisdom and their devotion might help them learn about Self and start their journey on the path of self-awareness.

843. The main goal of analysing our personality aspects' role in our daily thoughts and actions is to detect our idiosyncrasies and make proper adjustments in our mentalities, especially for addressing relationship problems more realistically.

844. As noted before, all the three personality aspects have both good and bad qualities. Of course, Ego causes more trouble and leads to badness more often than the other personality aspects. However, Ego contributes highly to our welfare in so many ways, too, especially for boosting our confidence and managing our defence mechanisms.

845. On the other hand, Self could cause trouble and badness, too. For example, instincts make us believe in certain ideals or convictions that are no longer applicable in our complex society. For example, imagine making investments merely

based on trust or intuition, rather than doing due diligence and studying all the risks and alternatives before committing ourselves. Marriages in the past worked nicely simply based on couples' trust and traditional habits. However, society is now too complex to choose a spouse and live with him/her before years of searching, testing, and contemplating.

846. It is not necessarily a good thing that we have been forced to be analytical and indecisive, but we have reached this point by the force of history (and human idiocy). Our sense of spirituality, which is a pure symbol of Self, is, nowadays, tainted, too, by all kinds of religious fanaticism and major corruption of clergies. Therefore, Self has its weaknesses for adapting to the newer social needs and survival.

847. The problems with Model are numerous, too, and beyond the scope of our discussions in this book. For one thing, Model has made people phony and calculating and we have a hard job separating true compassion from fake ones. The manipulating power of Model is infecting our lives and minds. Now, we do not even believe our leaders' words in politics, economics, or religions. They keep disappointing us out of stupidity, sheer arrogance, and hypocrisy.

848. Even in smaller scales, Model often loses its potency when people can detect our pretences if we are not phony enough or good at playing social games. This causes more mistrust, frictions, and resistance, because people want to challenge our phony personalities. Although many simpletons fall for other people's pretences, making Model look authentic is tough, nowadays. Everybody is becoming more sceptical about other people's attitudes and words. Thus, instead of trust, we now mistrust one another unless proven otherwise.

849. Model is too prevalent in modern societies, which means people are manipulating or cheating one another more than ever. Everybody is trying to show-off and portray an image of themselves that is quite unauthentic. At the same time, they should try hard to be convincing, too. Their hypocrisy

and deceits must remain hidden. This is hard, though, since everybody is learning to discount people's pretences, and because the trust level is declining fast in society.

850. Relationship problems are often due to partners' personality clashes. However, most people are unaware of the roots of personality clashes. They are unconscious of, or insensitive about, the deep interworking of their personality aspects. Of course, they also ignore the fact that they and their partners cannot change their personalities at will. People's unique personalities cannot be changed easily. Only self-awareness, partners' goodwill, and gradual modifications through Self and Model may help them save their relationships.

851. Using Model for its merits might resemble the role-playing methods prescribed by marriage counsellors. However, a fundamental difference exists between these two approaches. Using Model, for improving ourselves, would be based on partners' true convictions to learn about, and manage, their personality aspects. The idea is not to behave in certain ways or express love artificially just to satisfy one's partner. Rather, the main goal is to learn about (and manage) one's personality flaws. Model can help us play artificial roles or authentic ones, of course. Model might cause damage if it plays artificial roles, but it becomes useful when it is applied to reinforce our authentic needs.

Self-awareness for Boosting Our Relationships

A useful process of self-awareness and minimizing partners' clashes is to pursue the following steps:

A. Monitor the three personality aspects' roles in your mood and behaviour regularly. Learn how each aspect of your personality is driven by some motives or impulses, and then find out what their sources and natures are. You may apply the list of the motives in Appendix 3-A (at the end of Chapter Three) as a general guide.

B. Always remember that keeping track of the inner-workings and symptoms of our personality aspects is the most crucial step towards self-awareness.

C. Assess the integrity of your motives and decide if they are suitable for an enlightened person who does not need to play games or retaliate. Apply Self and Model to curb your selfish motives and improve your tactics for managing your daily routines.

D. After gaining sufficient self-awareness and confidence, monitor your partner's behaviour in terms of personality aspects s/he uses to communicate. The objective is to see how your partner is helpless in the face of his/her forceful personality aspects. Note his/her helplessness to change his/her behaviour. Remember that personality aspects, e.g., Ego, are triggered by inner forces (instincts, genetic, habits, impulses) and external forces. Instead of criticizing him/her for his/her defects, see if you can help him/her follow a self-awareness routine, too, (mainly by observing his/her own personality aspects).

E. If impossible to tolerate your partner, or if you are unable to convince him/her to pursue a self-awareness regimen, stop your useless struggles to save a tarnished relationship. Either learn to live with his/her imperfections or get out of the relationship in a most civilized and hassle-free manner. Stop retaliating and arguing.

F. Even when both partners have enough self-awareness and knowledge of the personality aspects, building functional relationships requires a continuous monitoring of partners' 'personality aspect clashes' during their encounters, then making proper modifications along the way. Furthermore, couples must satisfy all the other needs of relationships, mainly the matter of choosing the right relationship model for them. An important role of a proper relationship model is to minimize the frequency of clashes between partners due to their two uniquely built sets of personality aspects.

Chapter Thirteen
Relationship Guidelines

Some implied *principles* used to help humans manage their relationships, until recently. Whether it was tribal, religious, or cultural norms, some form of ethics and etiquettes prevailed. Those values, ordinarily informal but clear, guided couples to live in some form of harmony. Surely, those outmoded types of family structures are no longer applicable or useful in new societies. Yet, the big question is whether our socioeconomic choices so far have been rational for humanity's long-term welfare. In fact, we are facing many choices at this time about relationships' health and a social structure to support families.

852. We stand at the junction of history and should make a tough choice. We can choose to let society and relationships decay beyond repair or find a means of reversing the effects of our neglect during the last century or so.

853. We can get smart and choose manageable social and marital principles to match our natural needs. All we should do is to admit to some basic facts around us. We must admit that we no longer know how to relate to one another emotionally, effectively, and compassionately. People's pains and social chaos have been growing daily, since we ignore the current immense cultural deficiencies. Our interactions with family,

friends and colleagues have become increasingly incoherent and insincere due to people's rising idiosyncrasies. Families are suffering in terms of both child rearing and couples' abilities to relate in their relationships. Spouses growing oversensitivity and subjectivity are ruining their marriages' longevity. In all, our marriages are tainted quickly, as no Generally Acceptable Relationship Principles (GARP) exist to guide couples.

854. We have a choice and obligation as individuals and society as a whole to introduce GARP and emphasize on its main guidelines as briefly outlined in this chapter.

855. Mostly, we should agree that viewing 'relationships' as an independent entity (R-entity), like a 'business enterprise,' does not undermine its emotional importance.

856. R-entity is only a concept with the sacred task of reminding couples routinely that relationship needs are unique and not an extension of their personal needs.

857. R-entity can be viewed as a vital third party (the third leg of a tripod) in relationships to keep couples alert and objective.

858. A marital partnership is many folds more demanding and complex than any business partnership, because the cost of failure is much higher.

859. R-entity just provides the opportunity of bringing a similar level of discipline that exists in business to *relationships*.

860. We are all facing major dilemmas because: 1) Relationships have now become too complex, 2) we need companions more urgently than ever, 3) we have become less patient and more sensitive, 4) we have become too obsessed with love and happiness in the new era, along with an idealistic view of relationships' capacity to provide all these niceties.

861. Meanwhile, our level of patience has suddenly sunk vastly, especially in relationships, since we have kept raising our expectations from relationships and life, and since we have not yet realized the need for a higher tolerance in families to endure our vastly complex relationships, nowadays.

862. These two crucial ideas of lowering our expectations and raising our tolerance level in families should be propagated in society by any perceivable means as a cultural initiative, instead of letting movies and novels do just the opposite.

863. We do not realize that we have created more limitations for our relationships, in fact, by our exaggerated view of its high potential, especially for bringing us love and happiness.

864. Our options about relationships seem to be clear. They are:

- Keep fighting and struggling in relationships, or live in solitude, while sticking to some rigid perceptions of an ideal relationship.
- Learn to accept the new reality about relationships, lower expectations, fulfil as much of our personal needs outside relationships, bear some level of relationship flaws, and separate civilly when a relationship feels unmanageable.

865. The ultimate objective of a relationship framework and a set of principles is to *empower partners relate to each other emotionally, effectively, and efficiently (the three Es)* calmly even when many of their personal expectations cannot be fulfilled in their relationship.

866. Relating emotionally does not mean love, but understanding people's limitations, hurts, and innate inability to change, and our capacity to still show sympathy towards them.

867. People are oversensitive but lack compassion. Often they are careless and heartless themselves, but are hurt by their partners' simplest comments or inadequate attention. This is, of course, a symptom of their high Egos, too.

868. The complexity of relationships is easy to grasp when we appreciate the intricacy of human nature. We should realize how hopelessly helpless we are due to our psychological flaws and idiosyncrasies.

869. Family relationships will keep getting more complex and confusing. Thus, we must view and accept relationships in a

different light, as a temporary union. And we must learn to become humbler humans and modify our life values.

870. We should also view relationships as a dynamic routine that needs constant monitoring and modifications thru GARP to help spouses relate emotionally, effectively, and efficiently.

871. Not having a relationship sounds ridiculous to a majority of us who seeks a mate as a basic need. Both our instincts and culture keep forcing us to attend to this need actively.

872. In all, we must modify our mindsets to grasp and handle the special demands of relationships. The particular relationship model that couples choose must keep their communications and affairs manageable, while allowing them to handle their personal needs individually.

873. A couple relates actively by propagating positive emotions, effectiveness, and efficiency in their routines—the three Es.

874. Couples relate passively when they learn to live with bare expectations from their relationship, although it still remains manageable and functional. The three Es are necessary at some levels in 'passive relating,' too.

875. It is important for partners to know about the way they are 'relating,' if at all, and acknowledge it, too.

876. The lack of relationship principles (GARP), as part of our culture, is a serious shortfall that prevents partners to relate.

877. GARP will be an easy-to-read document for the public. It will list all the facts and guidelines about relationships in line with the social setting of the time.

878. A replica of GARP is available in two books by this author, *The Nature of Love and Relationships* and *Relationship Needs, Framework, and Models.*

879. GARP's objectives are explained in Appendix 13-A at the end of this chapter.

880. GARP can help partners understand and respect each other's boundaries and to recognize how humans' innate shortfalls are affecting their attitudes. Unfortunately, the present state

of relationships is mostly tainted by partners' phony roles, games, and retaliations—instead of being run by GARP.

881. The bottomline is that we must be willing to sacrifice in some ways to gain the peace of manageable relationships, and we should learn how to tame our Egos to accept and honour GARP.

882. GARP is urgently needed because couples are unaware of the scope of conflicts that their demand for large levels of both dependence and independence has created, nowadays.

883. We need a culture eager and capable to promote GARP.

884. The process of implementing GARP would require a lot of learning and adjusting. This would take time and patience.

885. Logically, a fair, sensible GARP must be adopted quickly by everybody for his/her own benefit. Yet, overcoming our old habits and urges to entertain GARP or new relationship mechanisms would be difficult.

886. Convincing people about GARP's benefits and using some guidelines to replace their hasty or emotional decisions would be a tough cultural challenge.

887. GARP might appear doomed at the outset by its attempt to introduce reasoning and formulate some radical principles about relationships. Reasoning in the pervasive emotional environment of relationships sounds too absurd.

888. GARP feels like a bizarre approach in a society where logic and objectivity seem to have lost their meanings long ago.

889. Then again, the idea of introducing GARP appears to be the only option left for humanity to reverse the deteriorating state of relationships and societies. People's familiarity with GARP would improve social mentality and relationships' health all in itself, though the ideal cannot be achieved soon.

890. Most of us, with manageable amounts of psychological flaws and destructive urges, would eventually realize the potential of GARP. Mainly, we should become more open-minded and realistic regarding our expectations from relationships by adopting GARP.

891. A main objective of GARP is to identify a practical balance between couples' personal needs and the relationship needs in the new era and define those boundaries in GARP.

892. As human beings, with the objective of reaching our deep potentials and tranquility, we are wasting too much time and energy on the petty problems of relationships. This is absurd and a sin. We have a choice to live happier within manageable relationships.

893. Partners usually question each other's logic regarding their relationship approaches and needs and ask each other "Who said that?" GARP can provide a point of reference (as an authority) for many contentious personal preferences that partners find arbitrary at the present time.

894. Obviously, the suggestions in this book have no value for those readers who believe the situation with relationships is fine as it is. However, for those of us who are tired of the existing atmosphere, we must prepare ourselves for drastic changes if we are really looking for tangible results.

895. The bottomline is that we need a framework to redefine and revise relationship principles in line with socioeconomic conditions in our modern society.

896. Unfortunately, it appears that only radical solutions might reverse the fast-deteriorating state of relationships.

897. Nowadays, the main questions for any person looking for a companion should be: 1) Do both partners grasp the risks and intricacies of relationships?, 2) have they developed the right mindsets for facing the inevitable setbacks?, and 3) are they enough mature, independent, and strong to deal with both the inevitable headaches of being in a relationship and when it falls apart?

Appendix 13-A
GARP's Objectives

The dozen main objectives of GARP are listed below:

1. *GARP can help us* **capture and propagate the features of a successful relationship.** It will provide the list of success factors in relationships, like the ones briefly noted in this book's Epilogue.[‡] It will show how a relationship thrives, what it achieves, and what we can expect from it. Thus, GARP replaces the arbitrary (subjective) rules and criteria that couples currently use for running their relationships or assessing its viability. These tools will bring objectivity back into relationships.
2. *GARP can help us* **realize our psychological limitations as human beings.** It can show how our personal quirks cause relationship chaos. GARP can enhance partners' sensitivities towards each other, harmonize their expectations from their relationship, and give them a practical perspective about the substandard setting of relationships.
3. *GARP can help us* **realize why individuals' psychological defects are not easily repairable.** It will emphasize on finding the means of circumventing and bearing people's defects as much as possible, instead of nagging or criticizing them. Some of the ideas discussed in this book about human psychology can be adopted as *principles* and included in GARP. For example, we can agree that, as a valid principle, 'People can hardly change themselves.' One reason is that personality change requires access to one's unconscious in order to change one's cognition. One needs extraordinary energy and spirituality to become a better human. A major

[‡] Relationship Success Factors are discussed in depth in this author's book, *Relationship Needs, Framework, and Models.*

principle in GARP might reflect that 'The prevalent positive thinking mottos that claim people can change themselves by will and boost their lives can hardly provide the spiritual conviction and gradual enlightenment required for mental adjustments.' Only ongoing meditation and awareness, to grasp our Self more tangibly, might achieve this goal.

4. *GARP can help us* **realize that the majority of people now perceive personal independence as their highest social value.** Thus, new relationship models and principles should be built around the primary fact that couple's demand for individualism and independence cannot be restricted in their relationships. This is a modern perspective after the advent of the women's lib movement and race equality struggles. Despite the common logical goal of seeking dependence in relationships, which is also in line with humans' instinctual need for it, our desire for independence is overwhelming all our thoughts and actions, nowadays. Therefore, GARP must support this general trend that is preoccupying people now. Then, for pursuing this basic principle consistently, a high demand is on people to plan their personal lives somewhat independently, too, by keeping their expectations, including financial ones, from relationships low, while also respecting the spirit of cooperation and teamwork more than ever.
5. *GARP can help us* **realize that a doomed relationship should be ended civilly and easily.** To insist on correcting the inherent personality flaws of our partners, or retaliating relentlessly to make them suffer, is futile and childish. Once we believe in GARP's objectives and other facts discussed throughout this book, we realize our partners' helplessness in terms of their personality flaws and perceptions. With this mindset, we might at last see the futility of our lifelong struggle to either change our partners to suit our needs, or retaliate in order to hurt them the way they hurt us. Partners might find GARP, and the idea of stirring objectivity into relationships, beyond their patience or capacity. In that case,

submitting to a friendly separation is their smartest option. Ending unmanageable relationships should be a natural and automatic process.

6. *GARP can help us* **recognize that the focus for correcting relationship conflicts is not our partner, but ourselves.** As reiterated in this book, the only way for managing our lives, including relationships, is to work on our own flaws diligently and honestly forever. We must commit ourselves to become a better person regardless of its likely benefits for our relationships. A partner's decision to be a better person and means of pursuing this arduous mission is a personal matter and challenge. Accordingly, partners must not press each other in hopes of making them a better person or saving their marriage. It would not work this way. Changing one's attitude is a personal challenge and needs conviction, which cannot be forced on someone. A decision to change lies only in the hands of each partner. Thus, our demands and retaliations only make the matter worse.

   The goal of self-awareness is to prepare a partner to curb his/her Ego, bear relationship flaws better, and accept his/her partner's shortfalls easier, unless the situation keeps deteriorating beyond tolerance.

7. *GARP can help us* **create a mechanism for handling our relationships, in particular for starting or ending them, without the need to depend on government or religious formalities.** The more comprehensive GARP becomes, and the more it is universally accepted by people, the less they need official or religious rituals. Instead, GARP should help couples discuss their relationship bottlenecks objectively and judge the rationality of starting or ending it. Relationships start based on goodwill and optimism, yet we may get tired of our partner and wish to leave him or her, which is usually a natural reaction and must be honoured by everybody. Yet, the main cause of separations, nowadays, is the absence of principles to guide relationships and to measure their health

regularly. If GARP can fill this gap, there would be no need to depend on bureaucratic, expensive, and time-consuming processes of governments to resolve our conflicts or, even worse, authorize our decisions for divorce!

8. *GARP can help us* **establish relationship norms that fit the socioeconomic profile of the current era.** It must also remain dynamic and be modified as humanity advances into more complex settings. All the evidences indicate that life and lifestyles will get painfully complex for many reasons. This is true even if we adopt an optimistic viewpoint and imagine that we would not destroy humanity and the Earth altogether within a few centuries, or even decades perhaps. Nonetheless, GARP should fit the requirements of the time. It must be dynamic and progressive in order to be effective. Partners' urges for independence, for example, is the theme of the present era. It has been only a few decades since we, especially women, have become keen about independence. It is now incorporated in all facets of social life, including relationships. Many other psychological developments and structural changes have occurred in society, including our expanding appetite for sexuality, compassion, consumption, and children's prominent role and demands in family life. They all affect GARP's format, but nothing overwhelms GARP's theme in the 21st century as much as partners' raw, demands for identity and independence do. Surely, nobody can predict that in a century or so we will not feel just the opposite, i.e., demand dependence more heroically. People might finally realize that real compassion needs some rules of dependence. Then, swiftly, dependence may become the new fad and reality as much as independence is nowadays. This would actually be a rational progression that the author believes will happen. It will reflect either the humans' final defeat and desperation for peace, or a higher level of human maturity, which seems a possibility, although so remote.

As discussed before, couples are still not quite aware of the conflicts that their prominent demands for individualism have caused. They are unaware of the scope of confusions that their demands for large levels of both independence and dependence have created in their relationships. They subtly expect relationships to satisfy their needs for dependency, while they pretend and shout independence publicly. The subtle urge for dependence, while insisting on independence explicitly and noisily, is a major hurdle in relationships in the new era. We all must realize that we cannot have it both ways; to eat our cake and have it, too.

9. *GARP can help us* **develop the guidelines for couple's teamwork.** GARP must be somewhat proactive in terms of suggesting the basic models and principles of teamwork and negotiating. Actually, GARP should be developed with the intention of enforcing teamwork. Couples need tools to help them deal with a large variety of conflicts in relationships. Instead of suggesting all kinds of untested models or ideas, however, GARP's initial guidelines should remain general and flexible, while more precise ones are developed and tested gradually. At least a few decades will pass before a well-crafted set of guidelines, especially for teamwork, is developed by experts and made available to couples.
10. *GARP can help us* **choose the right relationship model and pinpoint the compatibility factors between couples in order to minimize mismatches.** Partners can choose the right relationship model for them based on their needs and personalities by using GARP's guidelines. These guidelines might also pinpoint the areas of potential conflicts between partners according to the relationship model chosen. Instead of looking for compatibility factors, as attempted presently, GARP might suggest only those principles that would help couples *relate* effectively within the context of their unique (but organized) relationship. Preventing mismatches and pinpointing the wide range and areas of potential conflicts is

another objective of GARP. This is different from the task of finding compatible partners. The existing compatibility tests have proven rather inadequate for developing effective relationships so far, anyway.

11. *GARP can help us* **work within a uniform framework to assess our relationships and communicate objectively.** Psychologists and marriage counsellors can communicate amongst themselves according to these guidelines, instead of suggesting a variety of personal or unproven methods. The existing techniques are not focused enough for tackling the roots of relationship problems. Thus, another objective of GARP is to create a uniform framework and language for psychologists and counsellors. Uniformity will not only make the diagnosis and treatment of relationship conflicts easier and transferable amongst experts, but also reduce the level of confusion and frustration for couples when each expert suggests different solutions and none of them works, anyway. Couples are suffering in their relationships already and do not need any additional source of confusion. They need a universally tested system to help them one way or another—in or out of their relationships.
12. *GARP can help us* **view *relationships* as an independent, unique entity (R-entity), which is larger than the sum of the two partners in it.** R-entity, as a fundamental principle by itself, has to be included in GARP. The idea is to boost objectivity in relationships, instead of relying on subjective and unrealistic impressions of couples to define and manage their relationships based on their personal needs and Egos. Various features of R-entity are listed in GARP for clarity and application. Yet, other principles listed in GARP would support R-entity, too. R-entity is the nucleus for developing the relationship framework and its components. It is just the conceptual platform for us to boost our relationships.

Chapter Fourteen
Governments' Role and Legal System

In recent decades, laws and social mechanisms have been modified to handle only the *symptoms* of relationship failures, instead of the dire effects of changes in lifestyles and couples' mentalities. Courts have been involved in financial settlements and child custody battles with ineffective outcomes. Most of all, these legal mechanisms have not addressed relationships' unique needs and couples' growing expectations in modern societies. Governments have not yet dealt with the changes in people's attitudes, which are the causes of existing conflicts in relationships. Nonetheless, the repercussions of people's new mentalities, especially when terminating their once precious relationships, require immediate attention, not just by couples, but mostly by legal authorities.

898. People, governments, and social scientists should somehow come together to assess our relationship choices realistically and decide about humanity as soon as possible, because the state of relationships has gotten out of control already.
899. As a first step, we must decide whether we can continue to live without some form of principles and legal rules to keep families in a relatively coherent harmony in the new world. The answer in the author's opinion is a resounding NO.

Thus, the objective in this book has been to suggest a means of returning order and harmony to relationships, despite the gloomy prospect, nowadays, to succeed in this endeavour.

900. In particular, we should advocate effective social norms and values to cultivate a culture that supports humans' personal and social needs in a practical manner.

901. People should push the society and governments to make the needed changes in all social structures affecting people's relationships. With the help of social scientists, they must recommend relationship methods and a framework that can bring *objectivity* back into relationships. All along, the main mental adjustments needed for couples, as listed in Chapter Twelve (Point 809), must be propagated to guide the public in handling their relationships.

902. In particular, the prevalent ineffective social mechanisms, including legal systems, should be revamped to support the new social mentality and relationship needs.

903. The overall role for governments and people to adjust the required social mechanisms are outlined below:

- Support and propagate the idea of partners' individuality and independence.
- Support and propagate the notion of partners' financial responsibility.
- Support and teach details of the 'relationship framework' to the public.
- Support the idea of time-bounded relationships in legal channels.
- Support and propagate the idea of relationships being treated as an independent entity like a business enterprise. The concept of R-entity.
- Support and spread the idea of limiting the government role in relationships, e.g., financial settlement for divorce.
- Support, and participate in, all kinds of research to boost the quality of a universal 'relationship framework' and

GARP to replace the outmoded guidelines of religions and inefficient laws.

- Teach the new relationship framework and principles (GARP) at high schools.

904. Scholars and experts must find creative ways of informing the public about the flaws of our existing ways. They should do more research and be more proactive about changing couples' mindsets regarding relationships.
905. Once a platform is defined and accepted by sociologists, psychologists, and the public, modifying and expanding GARP would be an automatic process like all other social processes in progressive societies of the future.
906. People and governments are careless about the ambiguity, confusion, and damages (both financial and emotional) that the existing social mechanisms are causing for relationships and society as a whole.
907. Governments are busy with so many socioeconomic matters already to worry about relationship failures. Therefore, they just deal with the symptoms of this social chaos the best they can at a high cost to taxpayers.
908. Especially, governments' negligence about the high risks of the new culture for humanity is amazing and embarrassing.
909. Governments' minimal influence on relationship decisions would boost the concept of individualism. It will encourage couples' sense of independence, since the responsibility of taking care of their personal interests is left to them.
910. For example, the existing asset distribution mechanism at the time of separation is a silly copout. It has evolved in this manner only because courts are not equipped to make a fair assessment of relationship issues and financial assets.
911. If couples did not depend on courts to grant them financial compensation for being in a relationship, their calculating mentalities would manifest before starting their relationships and many couples would not end up in bad relationships

merely according to trust, good will, or romantic sentiments spread in new societies so irresponsibly.

912. With less government intervention, partners realize the need to be more proactive and blunt at the outset. They would try to find ways to protect themselves in case their relationship fails. They would exercise their authorities as independent individuals and prepare a *contract* that outlines their needs and expectations. It particularly provides the clear terms of settlement in case of terminating their relationship.

913. The concept of couples signing a relationship contract is not new or unromantic. In the older and more practical cultures and religions, a form of contract has aided couples for many centuries to stipulate their expectations and boundaries. It is only in the new cultures where most people are so romantic and consider signing a contract tactless.

914. Whether couples' decisions at the time of signing a contract would be perfect or lousy is irrelevant, since they must strive to remain alert, as independent individuals making those big decisions thoughtfully and responsibly.

915. Of course, couples can always rely on professional advice to prepare the right contract for them. In addition, when new mechanisms are in place, many standard documents will be available for couples to choose a proper relationship model and the type of contract that best suits their needs.

916. The governments' minimal influence makes couples smarter and more cautious about their relationships. This approach would change people's mindsets and attitudes. There will be less unsuitable relationships. And couples will stay in their relationships longer, as they have initially thought through the stages of their relationships realistically, especially the sad ending that most relationships must face, nowadays.

917. The modification of government role in relationships has the highest effect on the financial independence of partners. Rather than letting courts decide about the distribution of assets at the time of separation, partners should agree at the

outset, independently and objectively, on a system that fits their expectations and put it in their initial contract.

918. The public's welfare, societies' prosperity, and developing a healthy culture are the main responsibilities of governments. Thus, it also has a duty to support a type of relationship framework that can address partners' needs most effectively and efficiently. Governments cannot leave this crucial task to chance and hope that things would work out nicely on their own in the society.

919. The relationship framework, models, principles, and unique needs must be taught in high schools. There should be strict rules for passing these mandatory courses, which are more important than sex education and many other courses.

920. Governments should become a lot more conscientious and proactive in teaching people how to budget and live within their means. Governments' enthusiasm, nowadays, to push consumerism for strengthening the economy is coming at the expense of family destructions and social catastrophe.

921. The benefits of having a term in marriage contracts (for the automatic annulment) are substantial. Just to note a few, it will:

- Change the entire social mentality about relationships.
- Guarantee partners' primary needs for individualism and independence.
- Satisfy the innate urges of humans (for companionship and procreation) without unnecessary formalities.
- Free partners from feeling trapped.
- Keep partners hopeful about future and happiness if their relationship fails.
- Make partners smarter about life and their relationship needs and decisions.
- Increase partners' enthusiasm to learn and practice the 'relationship framework' and GARP.
- Propagate a progressive, productive mindset for partners.
- Increase love and cooperation in relationships.

- Enforce teamwork as a crucial role in relationships.
- Increase the longevity of relationships.
- Make children's lives less stressful and more predictable.
- Reduce stress in families and society as a whole.
- Reduce the sense of possessiveness and jealousy.
- Reduce the burden on court systems substantially.
- Eliminate the need for couples to spend outrageous legal fees and time in courts.
- Reduce the fear of getting into relationships and facing its hassles—as if walking right into a very likely ominous trap.
- Increase economic productivity and social welfare due to reduced stress and time wasted on relationship quarrels between partners.

922. Governments should also minimize their role in regulating, and ruling about, relationships. This would push couples to depend on themselves and teamwork to manage the terms of their contracts.

923. While governments should stay clear of direct interference with relationship conflicts substantially, they must support universities and scholars to develop GARP and a practical relationship framework.

924. Although many couples use nannies, the matter of raising children versus following one's career is still a sensitive matter these days. One way to settle this issue is to make the partner who insists on having children accept the main responsibility for raising them, while the role and degree of the other partner's involvement are negotiated in advance and recorded in the marriage contract as well.

925. The question of having kids at all would become even more crucial in the near future. It will become essential to decide carefully if partners are prepared and capable of raising their kids properly for the upcoming tough societies, instead of spoiling them with materialism and similar vain values.

926. Sometime in the far future, people might even be given a right to sue their parents for bringing them into this world or the way they have raised them. This would be a good policy for making people more responsible for creating children, who may suffer in dysfunctional families, corrupt societies, and polluted, hostile environments.

927. Making children must be a calculated decision by intelligent parents rather than a selfish act to enrich their own lives, or even for the socioeconomic purposes of governments.

The Timetable to Make Radical Changes

We have some choices to reverse the deteriorating trends in relationships, yet we must wait for some incredible events and conditions to take their natural courses. During this transition, a large number of radical remedies, like the ones suggested in this book are implemented gradually. Although the following timeline for an overhaul of relationships extends over many decades, every single choice and action in that direction would have some immediate benefits for everybody. Even our simple grasp of the points raised in this book and making moderate adjustments in our mentalities about relationships would help us promptly personally and towards a more progressive and effective society.

928. Unfortunately, the scope of relationship problems is not still pressing people enough to take serious steps. Or they just do not know what can be done to stop this madness growing in relationships. Therefore, the situation will continue to get worse before people begin to appreciate the urgency for changing their mentalities and approaches.

929. Meanwhile, couples' expectations keep rising not only from relationships, but also in terms of finding the right partner for themselves. Everybody looks for a partner with higher qualities than themselves and better than their past spouses.

This is a mathematically unattainable demand emerging in society. The matter gets especially impractical when they seek love in a partner who must be trustworthy, attractive, and intelligent, too.

930. In addition to the rising egotistical nature of humans overall, people would continue to have even a harder time to get along with the opposite genders.

931. People are not properly trained to be in relationships. They have been brought up to strive for happiness, and to them companionship is mostly another means of capturing that elusive happiness. They like to ignore that the hardships of life and relationships remain an inevitable reality regardless of their naïve expectations and slogans.

932. Therefore, for the next 40-50 years, gender equality wars and conflicts will escalate and prevent people from finding common grounds for negotiating their needs and lowering their expectations from relationships.

933. The deterioration will be measured by the rising divorce and separation rates. However, other indicators will confirm the downfall, too, such as people's rising stress in relationships and society as well as the rate of unmarried individuals in various age groups.

934. A divorce rate of over 75% will probably be reached in 2060s. Then, the alarming trends might start an initial social interest to study relationships more seriously and consider some radical solutions more systematically. Governments and scholars will get involved more actively.

935. Various types of research are needed to develop a practical relationship framework and principles. Surely, the progress depends on the global economic condition at that time, as it will deeply affect the state of relationships in the future. With the high likelihood of a global economic collapse and the demise of consumerism, relationship conundrums might become of secondary importance when people must focus on their basic means of survival.

936. On the other hand, economic gloom might stir some sense of reality into relationships. Couples might learn to revert to their traditional mentalities and lower their expectations from both life and relationships.

937. However, let us assume that we can succeed to continue with a progressive 'better managed' form of capitalism and moderate consumerism. We would most likely continue to grapple with new socioeconomic hurdles. Those shocks, like the debt crises in the fall of 2008 and the summer of 2011, will haunt us for many years, but then finally make us change our mentalities. We might learn that deregulation and fully 'free enterprise' lead to chaos.

938. Yet, considering humans' appetite for greed and corruption, we might be heading for major troubles. This means more relationship problems, too, due to dire economic conditions and uncertainties.

939. Probably by 2080s, with a divorce rate over 80%, the public will acknowledge the need for change. It will be a period of reflection and realizing that the roles and games that couples are playing and their erratic expectations (e.g., demanding both dependence and independence) are only hurting them. They will realize the need to adjust their expectations from relationships. Then, a relationship framework and principles proposed by scholars might find wide support.

940. Most likely, the need for independence and individuality will still be a dominant factor, and thus set the tone for the upcoming relationship guidelines. Nevertheless, we should make sure relationship principles fit the needs of societies satiated with emerging progressive norms. A foundation is created to coordinate the development and dissemination of relationship principles.

941. Aside from interest and patience, it will take couples a few decades to digest the need for radical changes and adopt a progressive mindset about relationships. More education is

provided to the public, mostly at high schools, to promote the relationship needs and framework.

942. By the end of the 21st century, people may eventually learn the art of being independent financially and emotionally rather than only pretending it. More natural communication, and less role-playing and games, will find common appeal in order to reinstate some trust and integrity in relationships.

943. It will take another couple of decades for people to feel at ease with the relationship framework and principles. The new mindset will gradually find full acceptance and some innovative processes and guidelines find universal appeal. Social mechanisms, including legal system, will be equipped to handle the new setup. This will bring us to the year 2115.

944. It will take 30-40 years for the relationship framework and principles to become a natural setting in society. This will bring us to 2150.

945. Good luck; that is the best the author can hope for. Yet, he would be thrilled to be proven wrong if by some miracle the state of relationships begins to improve much faster than the above depressing dates, *if any such luck is ever destined for this badly evolved, spoiled, and helpless humans!*

Epilogue

Yes, we should be concerned about the destiny of love and relationships. Neither of them can serve us the way we expect them to merge and make us happy. In fact, the more we seek love, the more our relationships are becoming unmanageable and painful. And conversely, the more we need relationships to sooth our loneliness, the less we can depend on love outside ourselves to accomplish our naïve ideals about companionship. Instead, we need courage to think more practically about the way we can relate to another person more effectively based on realistic criteria for success in modern relationships. Otherwise, we should actually be worried even regarding the destiny of humanity altogether, as satisfying our basic needs for love and relationships would only keep getting harder and feeling more excruciating.

Sadly, we seem to have reached an impasse, with cynicism and hope, about the potency of love to build our relationships. We worry about the future of families if personal and social mentalities are not revamped drastically, yet we hate to face the reality about our misperceptions of love and relationships and admit that our whims are incompatible with the format of modern societies and human nature overall. We still cannot stop pampering our optimism regarding love and relationships satiating our dreams and imaginations like magic.

Nonetheless, it seems that we are reaching the saturation point and the society will come to a standstill soon—where most of us fail to have even a relatively reliable existence or companion. Therefore, the question is how much longer we are willing to deceive ourselves with our idealism and letting 'love industry' keep fooling us with so much nonsense about love and modern humans' whimsical desires.

Relationships' Main Success Factor

Offering a summary of this book's discussions proved rather impossible, since almost all the nearly 1,000 points in fourteen chapters are highlights necessary for appreciating relationships' needs and maximizing their chances of success. These facts, trends, and choices have been extracted from a big volume of contentious relationship issues, after all. And they appear to suggest that the most important and natural 'success factor' is couples' abilities to learn about relationship needs versus their own in the new era, and then set out to align them effectively. Consider this advice the summary of this book! Nevertheless, the bottomline is that we have created a very complex world for ourselves with so little expertise or interest to find practical solutions for our dwindling marriages.

At the same time, now the incentives for being a *thoughtful* and *realistic* person is rising fast, considering our zeal to find happiness and love around an ideal companion. One thing is certain though: Our conventional use of Ego or Model to find and keep a soul mate is surely doomed. It has brought us only more loneliness and frustrations with no chance to fulfil the spiritual love we desperately seek. However, becoming a good and enlightened person to reach and enjoy that kind of love and happiness is a tough task as well.

Being 'good' mostly refers to well-balanced personalities that stress on Self with the least amount of Ego, as practical and humble humans in general. These individuals find a higher chance of building viable relationships, as they develop more control over their attitudes and expectations, and because they believe in the value of a good relationship that is driven by unselfish standards. Model dominance encourages phoniness and game playing, which hinder our chances for naturalness and goodness as well. Still, Model dominance is rather less destructive than Ego domination for building relationships. Of course, both Model and Ego have positive attributes as well, which, in moderate dosage, might assist us in building good relationships. In particular, Model can be useful in exchanging complimentary gestures and empowering partners' positive interactions when it is done properly.

Assuming that we can learn to become a bit less selfish, the next step is to become as natural as possible by getting rid of all those layers of phoniness, pretences, neediness, and games. We must believe that arrogance and playing games cause only more obstacles for building healthy relationships and finding happiness. Yet, becoming natural is a tough task, too, even if we knew how to do it. For one thing, we cannot overcome our habits and outlooks rooted in our subconscious. Our modern societies advocate only more superficiality, greed, and games every day. Now, even marriage counsellors make couples more unnatural by goading them to play phony roles for allegedly improving their communications.

To become natural, we should know who we are, which starts by gauging our needs and the authenticity of the motives behind them. We should value our independence and integrity seriously. We should find our life purposes, instead of only imitating others and accepting social values blindly. While respecting others and their choices, we should curb our desire for their approvals of who we are. Most people have difficulty accepting a simple, needless individual in their close circles;

therefore, we should learn to handle that obstacle without any grudges as well.

Some level of *enlightenment* can help partners in building successful relationships, too. 'Enlightened' mainly means that partners are aware of humans' innate limitations. Accordingly, they have sympathy towards one another, while they keep their expectations from their marriages sensible. They realize their own quirks and appreciate that their partners often behave based on some inner and outer forces beyond their control as well; so their behaviours should not be considered utter malice all the time. A major implication of being *enlightened* is that partners are smart and patient. They know how to apply their zeal for goodness effectively in their relationships, too, despite the common disappointments and occasional hostility between partners. This divine understanding also raises one's patience and compassion.

For becoming a good person, good genes and a healthy rearing background are most important, of course. Still, one's ability for self-analysis and leaning about one's idiosyncrasies and needs can help one become a good person eventually. The discussions in Appendix 12-A, especially, offer good insights for managing our personality aspects and a method for raising self-awareness.

Only a tiny group of people has genetic superiority, grows up in enriching environments, or turns into good-natured and enlightened humans automatically. For the rest of us, with bad or mediocre genes and meagre rearing conditions, becoming a good, enlightened person requires immense motivation and efforts. We must first learn to overcome so many of our rooted quirks and values through gradual self-awareness. It requires special courage, talent, and conviction to acknowledge one's deficiencies and pursue a path of self-awareness. The learning process is long and painful, since it requires new convictions against our phony values and lifestyle—our social addictions. Through awareness, we study ourselves, the interworking of our personality aspects, relationship needs and objectives, and authentic life values. Then, we forego some of our habits, prejudices, dogmatism, greed, and jealousy.

The concepts of being ethical and considerate (*good* and *enlightened)* is a noble and popular principle in our minds. We know that, for building an ideal relationship, partners should know themselves and their needs in line with the relationships' generic needs. Still, in reality, we often rush to blame others to justify ourselves intuitively. We merely refuse to think and be objective. Our logic ignores that relationship conflicts cannot always be our partners' fault. Our crooked logic and Egos have convinced us of our flawlessness. Some of us, in fact, believe to be saints. Some believe to know it all.

Therefore, we often react negatively towards other people's viewpoints and logic relentlessly. We strongly believe that our relationship problems are due to the badness and stupidity of our partners. Thus, relationship conflicts arise mostly from our hasty judgments and misperceptions regarding our partners, instead of realizing and admitting our own quirks. The hurdle is that even for seeing the roots of the problems, we should try sincerely to curb our Ego tendencies and focus on self-analysis and self-awareness, rather than making crude judgment and blaming our partners merely to feel triumphant and fulfilled. Revamping our mentalities is a tough mission, after all, almost as hard as asking a swimmer to unlearn swimming.

Nonetheless, seldom both partners can be good and Self driven, which means most of us should find better ways of relating by maintaining a good balance of all the three aspects of our personalities—with Ego contained as much as possible. Ego's force and motives should be rather controlled through ongoing improvements in Self and Model. More importantly, however, we need a relationship framework to help partners maintain an effective balance among the personality aspects of two married, psychologically distinct (and usually disturbed) individuals.

The Primary Conclusion

Starting perhaps only half a century ago, suddenly all the old relationship principles have gradually eroded along with the advent of the so-called progressive societies and mentalities. Those old principles have become obsolete considering the dawn of new lifestyles, women's new role in organizations and society, and other symptoms of human efforts to prove their independence and spirits. Personalities have changed and now people have become extremely complex without any expertise about dealing with one another effectively in the new settings. Individuals' needs have skyrocketed and their expectations from life and relationships have accelerated, yet their patience and morality have declined vastly. We have merely propagated arrogance, extravagance, sexuality, juvenile life philosophies, and unlimited artificial needs.

Anyway, at the end, the original conclusion raised in the Introduction and elaborated all along must be reiterated, as the message seems to have some type of urgency for humanity. The noted trends in Part II also provide a proper foundation for planning and building a healthy relationship environment urgently. Reading the whole book again, maybe a few times, could be a good strategy as well, to strengthen our convictions and revamp our naïve mindsets about relationships. At last, we might agree with the main fact, trend, and choice offered at the beginning of the book. That is, we must eventually admit that:

The Main Fact

Our understanding of love and relationships is wrong.

The Main Trend

Relationship conflicts have gotten out of hand
and the situation will continue to worsen.

The Main Choice

Only a drastic change in our mentalities can save the future
of relationships and alleviate human pains.

www.ingramcontent.com/pod-product-compliance
Lightning Source LLC
LaVergne TN
LVHW090944080826
845145LV00003B/880

* 9 7 8 1 9 8 8 3 5 1 0 4 9 *